Stroudwater and Thames & Severn Canals Towpath Guide

Michael Handford and David Viner

ALAN SUTTON
1988

Alan Sutton Publishing Limited
Brunswick Road · Gloucester

First published 1984
Reprinted 1988

BRITISH LIBRARY CATALOGUING IN PUBLICATION DATA

Handford, Michael
    Stroudwater and Thames & Severn canals towpath guide
    1. Thames and Severn Canal (Cotswold Hills, England)
    — Description and travel   2. Stroudwater
    Canal (Cotswold Hills, England) — Description
    and travel
    I. Title   II. Viner, D.J.
    914.24'17   HE437.T/

    ISBN 0-904387-61-5

Cover photograph of Ryford on the Stroudwater Canal by David Viner
Maps by Martin Latham.
Photoset Linotron Palatino 10/12 by
Alan Sutton Publishing Limited.
Printed in Great Britain

Stroudwater and
Thames & Severn Canals
Towpath Guide

STROUDWATER AND THAMES & SEVERN CANALS

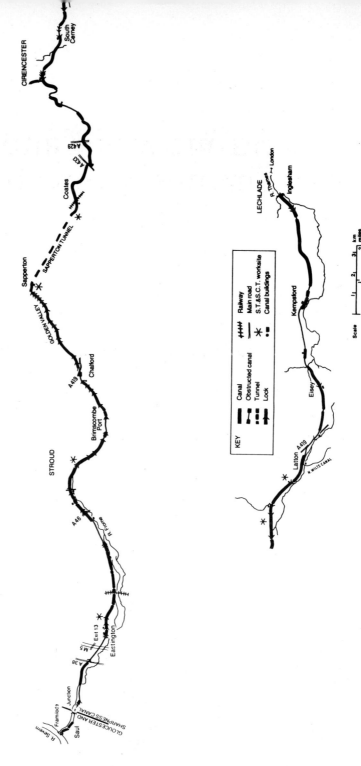

KEY

Canal
Obstructed canal
Tunnel
Lock

Railway
Main road
S.T.&S.C.T. worksite
Canal buildings

South Cerney
CIRENCESTER
A429
A433
Coates
SAPPERTON TUNNEL
Sapperton
GOLDEN VALLEY
Chalford
A419
Brimscombe Port
STROUD
A46
R. Frome
Eastington
Exit 13
M5
A38
Junction
GLOUCESTER AND SHARPNESS CANAL
Framilode
Saul
R. Severn

LECHLADE
Inglesham
R. Thames → London
Kempsford
Eisey
Latton A419
N. WILTS CANAL

Scale
km
miles

Contents

This volume is dedicated to everyone including the many un-named navvies associated with the Stroudwater and Thames & Severn Canals between 1729 and 1954. It is also dedicated to those imaginative men and women who working without payment or benefit to themselves are creating a new life for canals in the twenty-first century.

'. . . it ought to be remembered that there is nothing more difficult to take in hand, more perilous to conduct, or more uncertain in its success, than to take the lead in the introduction of a new order of things. Because the innovator has for enemies all those who have done well under the old conditions, and lukewarm defenders in those who may do well under the new. The coolness arises partly . . . from the incredulity of men, who do not readily believe in new things until they have had a long experience of them.'

Machiavelli *Il Principe*

Introduction

The idea for this volume stemmed from our own interests in the history of the Stroudwater and Thames & Severn Canals, motivated by the growing public interest in the future of the two canals. In response, we hope that this guide will encourage further activity and so improve the prospects for complete restoration.

We should perhaps explain first of all how this major revival of local and national interest came about. The navigable rivers and canals of England contributed a great deal to the world's first industrial revolution in the eighteenth and nineteenth centuries. Gradually pushed into the background by the railways from the 1820s onwards, canals suffered over a century and a half of neglect and indifference. From the 1860s the national volume of commercial traffic carried on inland waterways began its long downward trend interrupted only occasionally by temporary wartime boosts in trade.

By 1945 commercial traffic had long ceased to make any significant contribution to canal company revenues and pleasure traffic was still negligible. About half the network of canals was already abandoned and derelict. The remainder were ignored by government, local authorities and public alike. The canals were 'a problem' – largely inherited from the railway owners by an unenthusiastic British Transport Commission when the railways themselves were nationalised in 1948.

The first signs of change came with the formation of the Inland Waterways Association in 1946 with its commitment to the restoration and multi-functional use of all inland waterways in Britain. At the time it seemed an impossible and impractical dream but in retrospect has proved to be a turning point in the history of our canal system. Against all the odds, energetic I.W.A. campaigns helped save most of the heritage which remained although the Stroudwater Canal itself slipped through the net in 1953-4. Gradually public awareness of the existence and potential of inland waterways developed into ideas for all kinds of uses old and new: general recreation and amenity, a 2,000 mile long linear park, used for water supply and drainage, a unique working museum of industrial archaeology, access for fishing and walking and protected reserves for wildlife. The development of tourist potential with its associated job creation was also called for, with perhaps even a revived commercial traffic. By the early 1970s most government and many local authorities had come to accept that canals could be real assets to the community and no longer embarrassing liabilities. In that sense the 'problem', which had perhaps been no more than a poverty of imagination, had disppeared.

This developing national awareness of the potential economic value of inland waterways was paralleled by the formation of about a hundred regional and local societies concerned with specific canals. Some of the longer established groups have already been involved in successful restoration schemes – such as the Peak Forest and Ashton canals, the River Avon from Tewkesbury to Stratford, the Kennet and Avon Canal from Bath to Reading and the Basingstoke Canal from Byfleet towards Basingstoke. Both these latter are strongly supported by constructive local authorities anxious to capitalise on the enthusiasm, skills and fund raising abilities of well established restoration societies. A third major scheme is developing on the thirty-five mile long Montgomery Canal in Shropshire and Powys. There are also about a dozen smaller restoration schemes operating on the Pocklington and Market Weighton Canals in Yorkshire, the Droitwich Barge Canal in Worcestershire, the Cromford Canal in Derbyshire, the Monmouthshire Canal in Gwent, the River Stour in Suffolk and elsewhere. In addition a further dozen or so projects all over Britain are at the early planning and discussion stages.

More locally, this growing public interest led to the formation by Michael Ayland of the Stroudwater Canal Society in December 1972, which by 1975 had restructured its organisation to become Stroudwater, Thames & Severn Canal Trust Limited. Completed projects so far include the Eastington – Ryeford clearance, the renovations at Bow-bridge and (most spectacular) the imaginative restoration of the Coates portal of the Sapperton Tunnel. The Trust is currently restoring Cerney Wick lock on the Thames & Severn and dredging the long Stonehouse pound on the Stroudwater Canal. As a result, the canal restoration movement now enjoys a much closer consultation with local district and county councils, particularly for work on the Thames & Severn Canal. The Trust has been a significant contributor towards the public re-assessment of the future of these two canals, and we both hope that these changes in attitude will continue and strengthen.

We anticipate that this text will quickly become obsolete and require revision as existing and planned restoration schemes on the Stroud-water and Thames & Severn Canals are completed and new sections considered. As major restoration schemes are completed elsewhere in Britain, and as local and national interest in these two canals continues to increase, we hope that this important regional scheme will become a focus of activity, funded from a wide variety of sources, and leading to a completed restoration programme within the foreseeable future.

For the Thames & Severn Canal sections David Viner acknowledges the considerable contribution to this volume made by Edwin Cuss of Cirencester in text, ground survey and enthusiasm. For the Stroudwater Canal Michael Handford acknowledges the characteristic help of local canal experts Frederick Rowbotham and Lionel Walrond whose generosity, friendship and encouragement are much appreciated.

Finally, but not least our joint thanks to our publisher, Alan Sutton, who has patiently awaited completion of this volume during our various and separate commitments elsewhere. We, like him, hope that the popularity of this guide will ensure future editions and an opportunity to correct errors, revise entries and record the steady advance of the Stroudwater, Thames & Severn Canal Trust to its goal of uniting once again by canal two of the greatest rivers of southern England.

Michael Handford,
6, Spa Lane,
Hinckley,
Leics. LE10 1JB

David Viner,
8, Tower Street,
Cirencester, GL7 1EF

New Year's Day 1983

The publication of a second edition provides an opportunity to correct minor slips and errors in the text, although no attempt at a detailed up-dating has been possible. In the five years since the first edition was published, much restoration work has been undertaken on the canals and the towpath walker will easily identify this on his travels. However, a great deal needs to be done and the magnitude of the task is only too apparent to those who study the history of these two canals and examine the evidence on the ground. Our anticipation expressed in 1983 that the restoration programme for the Stroudwater and Thames & Severn Canals would attract the scale of resources and activity required for a successful outcome has yet to be fulfilled. It is easy to be pessimistic. However, much of the efforts of the Trust have been devoted to preventing further deterioration and loss of access and in responding to such major challenges as the Stroud East-West by pass which has changed the landscape of the town close by the canalside. Despite such challenges, it is with optimism that the walker (as indeed the historian, naturalist and angler) can continue to enjoy the towpath of these two canals and study their history over the past two centuries.

Finally, this new edition coincides with the opening of the National Waterways Museum in Gloucester Docks, bringing the wider canal story to our doorstep in a new and welcome waterways development.

MH and DV

St David's Day 1988

9

A Note on Method

Our main objective throughout this guide has been to provide details of the surviving remains of the two canals and particularly to improve knowledge of and access to the line of the towpath throughout its length from Severn to Thames. The accent throughout is on identification on the ground, and although historical details are given we recommend that the standard histories of the two canals be consulted as a matter of course. These are:—

> Michael Handford: *The Stroudwater Canal*
> Alan Sutton, Gloucester, 1979
> Humphrey Household: *The Thames & Severn Canal*
> second edition, Alan Sutton, Gloucester, 1987.

Other works of reference are listed under 'Further Reading' and we make no apology for quarrying material from a wide range of sources, thus reflecting the work of those who have studied the canals before us.

The text is a joint venture, with Michael Handford responsible for the Stroudwater and David Viner for the Thames & Severn. Each author remains responsible for his own section. We hope that, despite our individual styles, there is an acceptable consistency throughout, and the maps are presented in a uniform manner with a standard code. Points of access are noted where appropriate. Although perhaps the greatest satisfaction is to be gained by walking the lengths along which public rights of way exist from west to east (much to be preferred incidentally than east to west), we accept that most users of the guide will have less time at their disposal and will probably look at the canals in sections at a time, using their own or public transport to get to those sections. The general assumption has been made in the text that the route will be explored in a continuous manner from west to east.

Although the length of public footpath along the canals is remarkable in both mileage and visual attraction, we would also like to emphasise that much of the line remains in private hands and some stretches are particularly closely regarded by their owners. We cannot condone trespassing without permission and neither the authors nor the publishers hold themselves responsible for any infringements of trespass or indeed other matters which might result from the use of this guide. We have tried throughout to point out such ownership issues and where appropriate have endeavoured to contact and take advice from as many landowners as possible via the good auspices of the Trust. We are grateful for the advice of respective officers of the Gloucestershire and Wiltshire County Councils and the Stroud and Cotswold District Councils on footpath and other matters during the compilation of this guide.

Whenever possible we have supported the text not with up-to-date photographs of the route, which seemed to us unnecessary, but with material of some historical interest. Indeed, so rapidly have changes occurred along the line that even photographic surveys carried out in the 1950s and 1960s have provided useful historical information. It follows that both authors would be pleased to hear from anyone possessing similar material for either canal, in order to improve the record even more. It is hoped that users of this guide will themselves contribute to the record by photographing as they proceed and by keeping a log of subjects chosen, date photographed etc. The value of earlier such surveys lies not only in the photographs themselves but also in the meticulous care with which they were filed and listed.

For anyone contemplating a stay of several days in the area, details of local accommodation can be obtained for the western section from the Tourist Information office in Stroud (Council Offices, High Street, tel. 04536-4252) and for the rest of the route from the Tourist Information Centre, Corn Hall, Cirencester (0285-4180) which also has details of all local bus routes and other local services. Bristol Bus Co. (04536-3421/2), Swanbrook Transport (0452-712386 & 713857) and British Rail (0452-29501) will also supply information.

For displays on the canals and their history, we would recommend a visit to the Stroud Museum, Lansdown (04536-3394) and the Corinium Museum, Park Street, Cirencester (0285-5611). Although neither exhibition is particularly extensive (at Cirencester it is part of a changing programme of displays) both provide some feel for the subject as well as useful introductions to the region. Further afield, the Gloucester City Folk Museum, Westgate Street (0452-26467) displays a model of the weighing machine from Brimscombe Port. Each museum has at least one mileage plate from the Thames & Severn (whilst Cirencester has recovered a complete milestone) and one mileage plate can be seen in the Waterways Museum, Stoke Bruerne, Towcester, Northants (0604-862229) which is a must for all canal enthusiasts.

Finally, and in addition to the maps in this guide, we would recommend the use of the Landranger Series of Great Britain Ordnance Survey 1 : 50000 maps sheets 162 and 163 for both background and supporting information.

Stroudwater and Thames & Severn Canals Towpath Guide

1. *Framilode Lock and River Severn c. 1900. John White was then lock-keeper at Pike Lock. The capstan helped wind trows into the lock from the river. Notice the stone apron below the lock to protect it from powerful Severn tides and for trows to lie against waiting to enter the lock. The shape of the hand-rail and the circular gate paddle gear is typical of the canal.*

CHAPTER ONE

The Stroudwater Canal – an historical outline

The Stroudwater Canal was built between 1775 and 1779 from Framilode on the River Severn to Wallbridge, Stroud. It was constructed as a branch canal from the already navigable Severn to bring Shropshire, Staffordshire and later Forest of Dean coal to the prosperous woollen industry centred on Stroud. The woollen industry had originated at least seven centuries earlier as a cottage based domestic trade to supplement farming incomes and had thrived and grown over succeeding centuries. Gradually more and more of the woollen production processes were transferred from the home to adjacent workshops. By the mid eighteenth century some of these processes had gone a stage further and moved into separate purpose-built mills using machinery driven by the water power generated from the River Frome and its tributaries.

At this point in the history of the industry a number of crucial factors come together. Firstly, Stroud had developed into one of the earliest and most important industrial areas in a still largely agricultural England. As early as 1712 Sir Robert Atkyns considered the clothing trade so prominent in the county that no other industry deserved a mention, and his comment was equally apt for the rest of the century. The prominence of the woollen cloth industry in the county at this time was most apparent in the Stroud area where the town grew into a local centre for organising the surrounding villages and mills. Secondly, this industrial and associated population growth was placing increasingly severe strains on local fuel supplies based on neighbouring woodlands. Without a new source of fuel the industry would be unable to expand any further. This new fuel was coal available from the nearest pits in the west Midlands. Thirdly, the success of the woollen industry itself provided the capital for constructing a new type of transport which could bring in large, regular and inexpensive supplies of fuel. The woollen industry therefore created the demand for better transport facilities, the money to build it and the entrepreneurial expertise in the guise of local clothiers to bring the Stroudwater project to fruition.

It was these key men – numerous, influential, monied, respectable, organised and highly innovatory – in this dominent local industry who were the prime movers in all five attempts to build a canal to Stroud. This was a local canal built by local men with local capital for local reasons and not part of some grandiose scheme for uniting Severn and Thames.

The Stroudwater Canal is significant in the development of our heritage of inland waterways for a number of reasons. Together with several earlier waterways in France, the Exeter, Stamford, Newry and other canals in the British Isles, the Stroudwater stands in direct contradiction to the long disproved but still widely believed claim that the canal age began only with the opening of the Bridgewater Canal in 1761.

The inaccuracy is still repeated in the texts of a few poorly researched canal books and television documentaries. The Stroudwater Canal was first planned as a canal in the late 1720s and this makes it one of the oldest successful canal schemes in the country.

Secondly the canal never came into railway or public ownership like most other canals in Britain but is still owned by its original promoters established by the first Stroudwater Canal Act of 1730. Today the majority of the two hundred shares in the Company of Proprietors of the Stroudwater Navigation are owned by a small number of Trustees.

Thirdly, the visit of Frederick Louis, Prince of Wales, to the private canal built by Richard Owen Cambridge in the 1740s may be the earliest recorded use of a man made waterway in England for pleasure traffic.

Fourthly, the Kemmett Canal – an earlier version of the Stroudwater Canal – was built from Framilode to the Stonehouse area between 1759 and 1763. This highly unusual canal is the only known case of a waterway originally constructed entirely with cranes instead of locks to effect the changes in level. Finally the Kemmett Canal demonstrates the earliest known use of container traffic on any inland waterway.

The first attempt to build a canal developed in the late 1720s when a group of nine men, predominantly local men of wealth and social position connected with the woollen clothing trade, successfully applied to parliament to build a waterway. Their objective was to connect their town with the supplies of coal carried down the Severn, landed at Gloucester and Framilode and then carted by wagon and packhorse train to Stroud and cloth making villages like Stonehouse. Although the distance by road from Framilode to Stroud was only ten miles or so, this short stretch of land carriage proved a major obstacle for the Stroudwater clothiers. There were problems of supply and reliability when local roads like these were well known for their indifferent condition in the best of weathers and their occasional impassability during the winter months. There were problems of volume as the growing woollen industry wanted progressively larger and larger amounts of coal carried on this inadequate road system. Above all there were problems of price. Edward Owen, the Shropshire barge owner, sold his coal for 10s. 6d. a ton at Gloucester or 11s. at Framilode. By the time it had been carted to

Stroud the heavy extra cost of land carriage had raised the price to between 19s. and £1. 2s. 0d. a ton.

The promoters own calculations suggested that a canal would solve the problems of supply, reliability and volume as well as reducing the price of coal at Stroud to about 15s. a ton.

These substantial annual savings were expected both to pay back the capital cost of constructing the canal within a decade, as well as providing continued annual savings and a regular dividend thereafter. When the promoters also calculated the lower prices for other goods like corn, malt and provisions for their workforce it became clear to them that they could ill afford to delay this important transport innovation any longer.

Sometime during the late 1720s therefore, nine local men came together to promote an act of parliament to give them powers of construction. They approached John Hore of Newbury who had successfully made both the rivers Kennet and Bristol Avon navigable a few years before. Hore proposed a scheme for the Stroudwater Canal which included an eight and a half mile cut separate from the River Frome except where it crossed from one bank to the other, and twelve pound locks. The estimated cost totalled about £20,000 and the canal was designed to avoid interfering with water levels on the Frome and so affecting the power generated from water-powered mills on the river. The bill received the Royal Assent on 26 May 1730. It included powers to make cuts – clauses the proprietors were to hear more of in the years ahead.

However at this point some disagreement apparently broke out among the newly appointed proprietors. This probably centred on the group of nine mill owners on the Frome west of Stroud who had argued during the passage of the bill that any canal would take water from the river, reduce its flow and thereby reduce the amount of power they could generate. The opposition to the bill had led to the inclusion of potentially expensive damage clauses and it was no doubt these provisions which led the promoters to abandon this first attempt to build the canal to Stroud. For almost a quarter of a century after this the idea of a Stroudwater Canal remained dormant.

Shortly after his wedding in 1740 Richard Owen Cambridge settled with his new bride at the family seat of Whitminster House, Whitminster, on the banks of the river Frome. Cambridge spent a great deal of time reorganizing, landscaping and improving his large estate including making the river Frome navigable from its junction with the Severn at Framilode for nearly three miles as far as the Bristol Road (now the A38). Few details of the navigation survive apart from the visit of the Prince of Wales to Whitminster and his excursion on Cambridge's private navigation. There is no evidence of locks being built to bypass Framilode,

Whitminster or Fromebridge Mills and the suspicion remains that Cambridge may have been the first to use cranes instead of locks to effect the changes in level on the River Frome. Cambridge left Whitminster in 1751 and the canal probably silted up and returned to its natural state shortly afterwards. This unusual canal, which can still be seen in parts, was never envisaged as part of some longer waterway between the Severn and Stroud.

The second attempt to build a canal to Stroud surfaced sometime in late 1754 or early 1755 when John Dallaway of Brimscombe, a gentleman and wealthy clothier of repute, promoted a subscription among his friends and business associates to cover the cost of resurveying the river and calculating the probable cost of construction.

Once again the basic pattern of support for the canal remains comparable to the first attempt of 1730. All the supporters lived in Stroud or the immediate neighbourhood and all were men of position and substance mostly involved in the woollen trade. Dallaway employed three groups of engineers who included Thomas Chin, the noted Tewkesbury millwright and river engineer, Thomas Bridge, another Tewkesbury engineer, and most notably Thomas Yeoman, the well known engineer involved in later Stroudwater schemes. Dallaway proposed to make the river navigable using fourteen pound locks, two flash locks and cuts round every mill on the Frome. It soon became clear, however, that the virulent opposition from mill owners using the river for power generation was as active as ever and attempts to raise the estimated £10,000 construction costs were unsuccessful. The scheme was abandoned in June 1758.

At about the same time four Tewkesbury men – John Kemmett, Thomas Bridge, Arthur Wynde and James Pynock – proposed to build a canal to Stroud using cranes instead of locks to effect the changes in level and so avoid the opposition of mill owners incensed at possible interruptions to their water supplies. The four partners agreed to build the canal from Framilode to Wallbridge at their own cost. Once the canal was completed and operating successfully the canal company would buy the canal for £10,000. Since no difficulties were expected from mill owners if this design were used there would be no problems in raising the money this time. This unorthodox scheme involved widening and straightening the line of the River Frome using the millponds and millraces as navigation channels to bypass the mills. At each mill doubled headed cranes were installed lifting the cargoes in containers from boats on the lower level and swinging round to deposit them in other boats on the higher level. Parliamentary sanction for the new scheme was granted in April 1759 and work began soon afterwards. Although it is not certain exactly how much of the canal was in regular use, it seems likely that construction reached Stonehouse. Goods were damaged by repeated loading and unloading and, more seriously, continued handling meant transport costs were not competitive with even the expensive turnpike roads. The third attempt to build a canal to Stroud was abandoned in April 1763 leaving several of the partners in acute financial difficulties.

As the local woollen industry grew in size over the next decade or so, pressure for local transport improvements continued to increase. A further short lived attempt to revive the idea was tried unsuccessfully in 1768 but it was not until the opening of several other canals with links to the Severn, notably the Droitwich Barge and Staffordshire and Worcestershire Canals in the early 1770s, that the Stroudwater promoters made a further effort to complete their canal. Early in 1774 a meeting at the George Inn, Stroud, supported the scheme for a new cut from Framilode to Wallbridge. Engineers were called in once again and new estimates made suggesting a canal could be built for under £17,000. By this time the need for such a canal had become so acute that there were no difficulties in raising the agreed £20,000. Construction started officially on 30 May 1775 when the first stone of Framilode Lock was laid by William Dallaway.

Soon afterwards work was interrupted by scuffles between the Company's navvies and opponents of the canal who claimed that since work was proceeding under the terms of the original 1730 Act this only included powers to make new cuts and not to build the entirely artificial canal which Thomas Yeoman now planned. The dispute was resolved in August 1775 when a trial at Gloucester Assizes decided the Canal Company had exceeded their powers. Construction on the fourth attempt to build the canal had already been suspended before the trial.

By this stage the Company had decided to apply for a comprehensive new bill to enable it to build an artificial canal. The bill progressed through Parliament during the winter of 1775-6 and received the Royal Assent on 25 March 1776. The new Act gave the Company powers to raise £20,000 in shares plus a further £10,000 if necessary. Work on building the canal restarted at once and the canal was open to Bristol Road by December 1776, to Chippenham Platt by January 1778, to Ryeford by January 1779 and finally to Wallbridge, Stroud, on 21 July 1779.

The cost of this fifth and final attempt to build the canal was about £40,000 – more than double the estimate – and this put a heavy strain on Company finances. For several years after the canal was opened the Company concentrated its resources on paying debts, building lockhouses, wharves and warehouses and generally improving the facilities for commercial traffic. It was not until April 1786 that the first dividend of 5% was paid. When completed the canal was about eight miles long with twelve locks broad enough to take Severn trows which traded on the river. Since there was no horse towing path on the river until 1811, the canal was also built without one. The usual method of towage was by men until 1825-7 when a horse towing path was finally built on the canal.

In April 1781 the Company took the first steps towards creating a Thames & Severn Canal Company. The Thames & Severn Canal Act was passed in 1783 with Stroudwater support, although it is interesting to note that few Stroudwater directors or shareholders were prominent financial supporters to the new company. Provided the new canal terminated at Wallbridge, the Stroudwater Company were not seriously interested in involving themselves in a costly and speculative project, especially while their own financial position remained unresolved. Once the Thames & Severn Canal was opened in 1789, the Stroudwater became part of a through route, and while the volume of through traffic over Sapperton summit was never substantial, the extra trade up the Frome valley to Chalford and Brimscombe benefited the Stroudwater tolls a great deal. The Company tolls of 3s. 6d. per ton were soon providing a profitable income. The volume of cargoes, the income from tolls and the level of dividends continued to rise during the rest of the eighteenth century.

Proposals for the Gloucester and Berkeley Canal in the 1790s were finally approved by the Stroudwater Company after a good deal of hesitation based on a fear of losing trade.

The agreement between the two companies provided for a junction a few yards south of the original Stroudwater line, a new lock (Junction Lock) so that the two canals could cross on a level, and the pound from the junction to Whitminster Lock raised. The depth of Whitminster Lock was thereby reduced to only a few inches. Since the Gloucester and Berkeley Canal ran out of money several times on its construction south, the new junction and lock at Saul were not completed until 1826.

Traffic, income and tolls continued to build up in the first decades of the nineteenth century, although the main source of the coal trade which comprised the bulk of all cargoes gradually shifted from Shropshire and Staffordshire to the Forest of Dean. Coal cargoes grew from 10,745 tons a year average around 1810 to 22,529 tons by 1822 and in the same period coal tolls doubled to £2,925 a year. The opening of new canals like the North Wiltshire in 1819 and the Gloucester and Berkeley in 1827 provided extra links and new sources of trade. Dividends climbed steadily from 8.7% around 1800 to 21% by 1824. By this stage the Stroudwater Canal was established in one more unusual role. It was by far the most profitable canal in southern England – an area already noted for the poor financial returns paid to waterways investors.

These comfortable profits were evidently resented by some local coal users who argued, with some justification, that Stroudwater tolls per mile were high by national standards. Railway interests combined with these coal users to promote a Stroud and Severn Railway from Framilode to Stroud parallel to the line of the canal. It is not clear whether the real intention was to build a railway or merely to frighten the Canal Company into reducing its tolls. In any event the Company reduced their highest toll from 3s. 6d. to 2s. 9½d. and shortly afterwards to 2s. 6d. per ton whilst at the same time mounting a vigorous opposition to the proposed parliamentary bill. The bill was defeated in May 1825. Although the original toll was restored for assorted goods a few years later, the lower toll was continued for coal and all charges were abolished for warehousing, wharfage and cranage.

The opening of the Gloucester and Berkeley Canal to Sharpness in 1827 brought further trade to the canal. In the hope of encouraging more long distance traffic, the Company began to introduce toll reductions on specific cargoes called drawbacks. These included a half-toll on flour milled from corn which had already paid a toll, and on items like iron goods from Gloucester and salt from Droitwich. Dividends reached over 26% by 1835. There was also a considerable temporary increase in cargoes during the construction of the Great Western Railway, but this ceased when the line was opened through Stroud in 1845.

The immediate impact on the Stroudwater Canal was marginal compared to the greater effect on the neighbouring Thames & Severn Canal Company who unsuccessfully proposed an amalgamation. Total trade on the Stroudwater continued to increase for about a further twenty years, though the Company had to accept progressively lower tolls as the effects of railway competition became more intense.

The Stonehouse and Nailsworth Railway Act was passed in 1863 and the Stroudwater Company found itself squeezed by falling income from lower and lower tolls as well as the first serious evidence that its remaining traffic would begin to fall away as well. A small income per ton from heavy traffic had been almost as good as the large income per ton from the lighter traffic of earlier years. By this stage the future promised only a smaller and smaller income from lighter and lighter traffic. Dividends dropped from nearly 23% in 1844 to 16% by 1853, 11.7% in 1865 and 5.3% in 1880.

Squabbles with the Thames & Severn Canal Company now clouded the horizon too. The Stroudwater Company had agreed to allow lower tolls for cargoes passing on to the upper canal in 1783. Now, with traffic and maintenance on the Thames & Severn Canal declining, it employed Edward Leader Williams, engineer to the Severn Commissioners, to survey the neighbouring canal. He agreed with the criticism made by the Stroudwater Company but no improvements seem to have materialised on the Thames & Severn. The Great Western Railway, which already controlled the Thames & Severn, discussed selling the canal to the Stroudwater Company in 1888 but their small offer of £3,000 was rejected. When the canal passed to the original Thames & Severn Canal Trust and later the County Council, the Stroudwater Company contributed £150 a year to try and keep it open. Decades of poor maintenance, falling commercial traffic, the absence of any substantial pleasure traffic or alternative sources of income and declining public interest finally led to the partial closure of the Thames & Severn Canal in 1927, and complete abandonment in 1933.

Meanwhile traffic on the Stroudwater Canal continued to fall over the long term. The last dividend was paid in 1922 and although some effort was made on arrears of maintenance in the mid 1920s, the canal was semi-derelict by the beginning of the Second World War. The last commercial toll was paid early in 1941, and the canal was eventually abandoned by Act of Parliament in 1954. Since then the income from property and the sale of water has enabled the Company to survive and pay its way. It is now assisting the Stroudwater, Thames & Severn Canal Trust to restore the canal between Eastington and Ryeford.

CHAPTER TWO

Upper Framilode to Saul Junction

The best way to get to Framilode to the catch the regular and inexpensive Swanbrook bus service which runs six days a week from Gloucester bus station directly opposite the railway station. The bus station enquiry office, ever anxious to provide a service to the public, does not provide details of Swanbrook times but fortunately these are available on a nearby display board or from Cheltenham (0242-32591). Better still buy the superb Cotswold Bus and Rail Guide published by an imaginative county council and available from enquiry offices (even Gloucester), bookstalls, newsagents, bookshops. There are several places near the towpath of both canals where bus or train services run back to Gloucester or on to Stroud, Chalford, Kemble and Cirencester, so it is easy enough to walk the two canals leisurely over four or five weekends using public transport services. The eight or so miles of the Stroudwater Canal can provide an easy and unhurried first weekend. The other alternative is to take your car to Upper Framilode and park it either facing the river opposite St. Peter's Church or in the Ship Inn car park if the landlord gives his permission.

The best place to start your towpath walk is on the Severn river bank opposite the church. Looking at the River Severn now with its huge tidal range, fierce currents, rapid changes in flow and numerous sand banks it is·difficult to believe that this was once one of the busiest and most important commercial water highways in Europe. Standing on this spot a little over two hundred years ago when the Stroudwater Canal was being built you would have noticed those specialised Severn craft, the trows,[1] plying up and down the river. These boat men used the ebb and flow of tides and their masted sails to assist the passage of their craft. Another technique was for men to push the trows upstream as they stood in the shallower waters of the river edges. It must have been an unenviable task in fair weather, let alone the depths of winter

From your left the trows would bring groceries and general merchandise up from Bristol and elsewhere. From your right trows would be carrying mostly coal and manufactured goods from Shropshire, Staffordshire and the Midlands. Many of these cargoes would be unloaded

1. The 'o' is pronounced as in 'throw'.

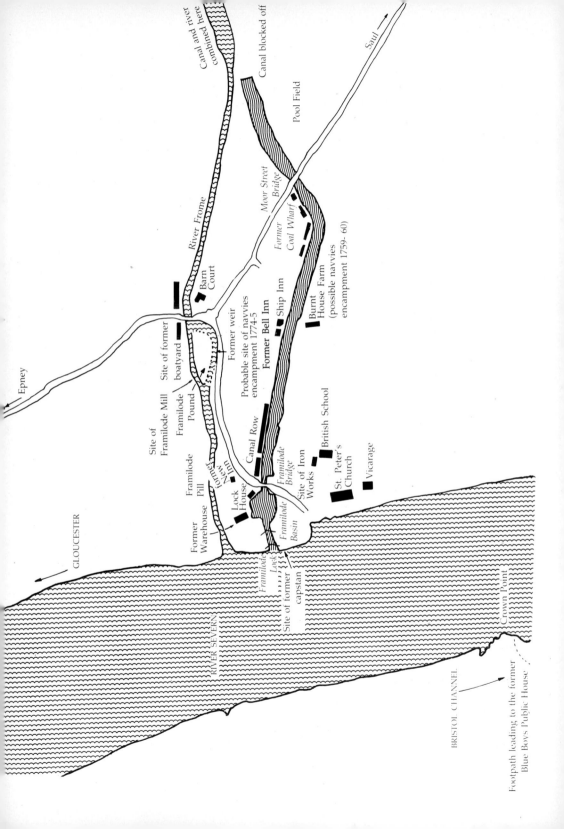

EPNEY

GLOUCESTER

RIVER SEVERN

River Frome

Canal and river combined here

Canal blocked off

Saul

Pool Field

Moor Street Bridge

Former Coal Wharf

Barn Court

Site of former boatyard

Former weir

Probable site of navvies encampment 1774-5

Former Bell Inn

Ship Inn

Burnt House Farm (possible navvies encampment 1759- 60)

Site of Framilode Mill

Framilode Pound

Framilode Pill

Former New Inn

Canal Row

Framilode Bridge

British School

Former Warehouse

Lock House

Site of Iron Works

St. Peter's Church

Vicarage

Framilode Lock

Framilode Basin

Site of former capstan

Crown Point

BRISTOL CHANNEL

Footpath leading to the former Blue Boys Public House

in small quantities at riverside villages like Framilode although larger settlements such as Gloucester or Worcester took greater quantities. Locally coal was unloaded on the river bank in front of the present Darell Arms at Lower Framilode where Thomas Cullis had his coalyard, and at Framilode Pill where the Frome runs into the Severn. Cullis' son-in-law, Richard Hall, kept the coalyard by the Pill and lived at the nearby New Inn. Some indication of the amount of coal landed here comes from John Dallaway who reported that about 3,700 tons of coal were sold at Framilode and adjacent wharves in 1754. Only about 700 tons were used for local domestic consumption. The remainder was carried by carts and packhorse trains to the growing settlements of Stonehouse, Stroud and nearby villages to supply their thriving woollen industries.

There might be other craft on the river as well. Perhaps one of the larger vessels, called 'brigs', was sailing by. These traded longer distances than the river based trows and were essentially sea-going craft. They carried cargoes to and from the South Wales ports, round Lands End to London and as far away as Portugal bringing timber and transhipped wine to the towns and villages of lower Severnside.

On the other side of the river an observant sightseer might see a small band of travellers walking down the path from the former Blue Boys public house (now a private residence) to Crown Point almost opposite the place you are standing. From here Thomas Cullis ferried them diagonally across the river in his passage boat to the Passage House at Lower Framilode where his wife Mary provided food, refreshment and accommodation. The Passage House and coalyard are long since gone, but the Darell Arms on the same site continues the tradition of hospitality. There was even a remote chance an unwary traveller might see one of those infamous craft which visited the Severn estuary with a press gang aboard, waylaid the boat men and mariners and carried them off against their will, from their wives and families to serve in a navy considered brutish even by the standards of the time.

Framilode itself – the lode on the River Frome – is evidently a village of some antiquity with long standing river associations. Although most of the houses in the village date from the late eighteenth and early nineteenth century, and have strong links with the growth of canal trade, the history of Framilode as a small riverside port distributing goods arriving by river to the surrounding countryside is a much older one. A beam at Barn Court, probably the oldest house in the village and certainly built before 1680, is marked 'certified accommodation for six seamen'. The roof is supported by other beams made from ships' timbers.

There is evidence too of earlier settlement in the area. Apart from a long standing suspicion that Framilode may have been the site of a regular Roman crossing of the Severn, excavations in the fields between Upper and Lower Framilode undertaken a few years ago suggest an early medieval settlement for salting fish and meat. A full scale investigation here by professional archaeologists could yield important evidence on the early history of the county.

Although it has been substantially altered several times over the centuries, the Mill House at Lower Framilode dates from around 1690 at the latest. The mill itself is much later. It was built c.1840 when grain was brought from Sharpness, discharged on the big pier which stood in front of the Darell Arms and transferred from there by a small tramway to the flour mill. Tom Ayliffe, who lived at the Mill House from around 1905, was the last person to operate the mill. He used his own boat, the 'Irene', to carry grain from Avonmouth.

At Upper Framilode there is firm evidence that as early as 1730 Walter Yate, the occupier of Framilode Mills on the Frome, considered his buildings were 'ancient Mills . . . ' and from this we can presume there must have been some cottages in the area providing homes for the small workforce.

The church at Framilode and the adjacent vicarage were built by the Darell family in 1853-4 to provide religious services for this thriving canalside village. Notice the many boatmen graves in the churchyard. The church key is available from the former vicarage to the right as you face the church. Cynics have long suggested that these were built to dissuade boatmen from using the church patronised by the Darell family. Since most locally based boatmen considered themselves 're-spectable mariners . . .' and bearing in mind any rougher element was unlikely to include regular attenders of any church – especially an Anglican one – this seems unlikely.

Both church and vicarage are well built rather than jerry-built shacks hurriedly thrown together to divert the religious zeal of Framilode boatmen from the gaze of the Darell family. The provision of a school by the family at the same time is evidence enough of a generous approach to supplying facilities considered essential by a local philanthropic family. The school still stands behind the church though it is now converted to a private house.

Turning from the Severn riverbank and walking back towards the village you will notice a group of modern detached houses on your right. This area was formerly occupied by a group of nine terraced cottages one of which was partially converted to a small village shop patronised by canal and river craft. The village water pump was also located here.

A few yards further on you will come to the canal itself and the site of Framilode Swing Bridge. If you stand on this bridge site and face the river you will see an infilled area originally occupied by the canal basin. At the far end of the basin area near the river are the remains of the substantially built Framilode Lock, constructed to withstand the powerful erosive effects of Severn tides. The basin and lock area are in private grounds and should not be visited without permission from the owners who live in the former lockhouse and warehouse. In any event it is essential to proceed with great care. The large cut stone blocks forming the end of the lock and the wall protecting the basin area on both sides are far from secure. It is all too easy to lose a footing in a hole covered with a superficial matting of grass and plunge headlong onto the hard river bed. As far as the basin and buildings are concerned the new owners are reported to be aware of their responsibilities of owning an historic site of public interest. There is little likelihood the basin will be strong enough or dry enough to be built on for many years to come and by then restoration of the original basin may become a possibility.

To the right-hand-side of the basin stand two buildings built by the Canal Company over two hundred years ago. The two storey building nearest the river and backing onto Framilode Pill was originally built as a single storey structure about 1780, soon after the canal was opened. The lower storey bricks are thought to originate from Frampton. Although it is commonly referred to as a warehouse it was rarely used for storing goods brought in by river or canal. More commonly the ground floor was used for storing sails, rigging and the like essential for navigating the Severn but superfluous for carrying goods on a barge canal. This equipment was kept in the building while the trow or other craft delivered its cargo along the canal and then recovered as the vessel left Framilode Lock again bound for the Severn. A brief examination of the structure of the building and brickwork confirms that the first storey with its two access staircases was built at a later date probably before 1800. These bricks are thought to have come from Stonehouse. This upper storey was used as a meeting room by the Framilode Friendly Society of Watermen and may have been constructed specifically for that purpose with funds provided by members. The warehouse is only one of two or possibly three which remain along the canal line. The warehouse has been renovated and converted into a private residence. The windows and side doorway are new but the original front doors, with their carvings of initials and boats, remain.

The Framilode Friendly Society of Watermen, reputedly founded by the retired master mariner Captain Charles Philip Butler in the 1830s, could have a much earlier origin as a river based friendly society for mariners and merely have been reorganised by the captain. The annual three day 'feast' of the Society began with a meeting of members each Whit Monday and continued until the following Wednesday. It involved a variety of events including a procession led by a band round the village with members wearing red, white and blue rosettes and carrying staffs decorated with flowers. The procession marched through Saul to a church service, originally perhaps at Fretherne or Frampton but later probably at the new church in Framilode. This was followed by a picnic meal held round the basin with food handed round on trays or a more formal meal in the meeting room using two large furnaces kept on the ground floor for cooking the hams. Each member wore his best clothes and used his own set of cutlery and crockery. The crockery incorporated an interesting circular design in the shape of a boat man's trouser belt. Wives and families joined in the celebrations which were followed by dancing on and around the bridge to the accompaniment of fiddles and accordians.

The Society flourished as canal trade grew during the first seven decades of the nineteenth century reaching a peak of about a hundred-and-forty members. Later on the Society seems to have experienced a decline. By 1916 numbers were down to about seventy or eighty people at the annual meeting and the church cerremony and procession had been abandoned. As trade shifted gradually from the canal and few younger men became boatmen or mariners the membership grew progressively more elderly and the meetings more sedate. Although the Society continued for a few years after the First World War it was soon afterwards dissolved and its members transferred to the Conservative Benefit Society.

The lock house, built by the Canal Company in 1815, faces Framilode Basin and is a typical example of Georgian vernacular architecture in this area. It was recently listed by the Department of the Environment although two similar buildings at Chippenham Platt Wharf at Eastington and Ryeford Double Locks as well as the equally significant Framilode warehouse itself still await attention.

The small extension on the lock house here may originally have been a carpentry shop used while the original lock gates were being constructed, though it was later converted to a sub post office in the nineteenth century. Locals maintain that bricks for the house and ground floor of the warehouse were brought in by river probably from brickyards at Frampton. All the land between the road, the Severn riverbank and Framilode Pill as far back as the lock house rear gardens was called Kemmett's Orchard. It belonged to John Kemmett whose ill-fated Kemmett Canal started where the Frome joins the Severn.

The remains of Framilode Lock at the far end of the basin are just visible from the bridge. It was a massive structure built of expensive but very hard stone from Guns Mills in the Forest of Dean brought down the Wye on barges and then shipped across the Severn. Begun in February 1775 to a design produced by Samuel Jones of Boston, Lincolnshire, it was excavated by navvies supervised by John Gleave and Robert Perry.

The first stone was laid by the Company Chairman, William Dallaway, on 30 May 1775 and the stonemason Thomas Barlett completed all the stonework. The carpentry work, undertaken by John Pashley with timber from Bristol, was completed by August 1776. The dimensions were 70' long, 16' 2" wide – large enough to take most Severn trows. The completed lock cost the Company an unprecedented £1,500 compared with the estimate of £700 and £400 for each other lock.

Just below the bottom gates of the lock on the downstream side of the Severn the Company erected a capstan to enable trows to enter the lock safely without being damaged by the fast river currents. Trows coming down the Severn usually turned and approached the lock from below so that they faced into the current and could control their craft more easily. Boatmen then either sent a towboat ashore with a line, scrambled up the bank themselves near the church or threw a line to the waiting lock keeper who tied it round the capstan, winched it in and eased the trow into the lock. When commercial traffic was at its height the lock was lit by lanterns at night to guide approaching craft on the river.

Turning round and facing up the canal from the basin you will see a line of cottages on your left running parallel to the canal on the towpath side. These are called Long Row or Canal Row and are reputedly built of local bricks perhaps from the old brickyard at Baldwins Farm, or more probably from clay dug out of the line of the canal. Several local people suggest these buildings were originally erected as warehouses to store tin used in Framilode Mill tin works at the time and in the small tin works originally located in the area occupied by the modern detached

2. Framilode basin and lock c. 1900. The two figures are presumably canal staff using the Company-owned rowing boat. The 'Rose', believed to be a tar boat, carried waste from Stroud Gas Works.

houses. It is more likely they were built soon after the canal was started as housing for boat families since they are not marked on a map of Carter's Close *c.* 1775 shown on page 32. Personally, I suspect they were financed by Richard Hall, under-surveyor and junior clerk to the Canal Company from December 1774 to April 1776. He kept the New Inn at Framilode (see below), was married to Thomas and Mary Cullis' daughter and worked as steward to Lord Ducie. There is no evidence for this, however, or any known reason why the cottages all faced away from the canal. The Canal Company charged 1s. a year for each house to take washing water from the canal and a further sum, usually 2s. 6d. a year for each window overlooking their property. The few windows now facing the canal are nearly all modern additions to the cottages. The first house on the canal bank nearest the bridge was reputedly built for the Canal Company foreman in 1776-7. The single storey structure adjacent to it could have served as a storeroom for tools and materials, as a stable or even as temporary accommodation until the housing at Long Row was completed. Notice that this house and the others in

3. Framilode Swing Bridge c. 1935. From left to right the warehouse, lockhouse and house believed to have been built for the resident engineer c. 1775.

Canal Row are all built of large bricks. We are hoping detailed research on brick history will enable us to date these houses more accurately.

The land occupied by Canal Row and the modern detached houses to your right was originally called Carters Close. It was here in the summer of 1775 that the well-known Battle of Carters Close occurred. Canal cutters employed by the Company earnestly dug out the canal by day while the canal's opponents, led by the ironmaster John Purnell of Framilode Mill, desperately filled it in again under cover of night. Frequent violent skirmishes are reported to have occurred to try and secure mastery of the Close before the rights and wrongs of the dispute were settled at Gloucester Assizes in August 1775.

The bridge at Framilode was originally a wooden swing bridge, but this was replaced in 1886 by an iron swing bridge, identical to many others installed by the Company at the same time. Several of these iron replacement bridges remain in position most notably at Saul Junction. The best photograph of the Framilode bridge is reproduced on the cover of *The Stroudwater Canal*. This photograph also shows a small winch and chain immediately above the bridge on the towpath side. This was used to lift a single stop gate which normally lay flat on the bed of the canal. It was raised in times of unusually high Severn water to prevent river floods backing up the canal, damaging the banks and inundating surrounding dwellings and fields. A small winding hole on the offside bank opposite the winch is now covered by the garden of the modern house at 1, Riveredge, Framilode. It is just visible on the extreme bottom left in the same photograph.

Leaving the bridge area and canal line for a short time, it is worth-while following the road on into Upper Framilode village leaving the lockhouse on your left and Canal Row on your right. Almost immediately you will notice an attractive slate-roofed dwelling on your left, part of which has been covered with plaster and the other part carefully restored to reveal its original timber framing. This is the former New Inn which was kept by Richard Hall during the period the canal was being constructed at Framilode. He was second clerk and under surveyor to the Canal Company for a short time and kept the accounts of traffic entering and leaving the lock together with the tonnages paid until the lock house was completed and the job taken over by Samuel Collins Jnr. He was paid a salary of £50 a year which, together with his coal business based on Framilode Pill behind the house, the revenue from the New Inn, his surveying interests and employment with Lord Ducie must have provided him with a more than comfortable income.

The left-hand-side of the building (now The Cottage) was the dwelling house and the right-hand-side (now Fromeside) incorporated the snug and jug and bottle department. The Canal directors occasionally met here and dined at Company expense while the Canal was being built in

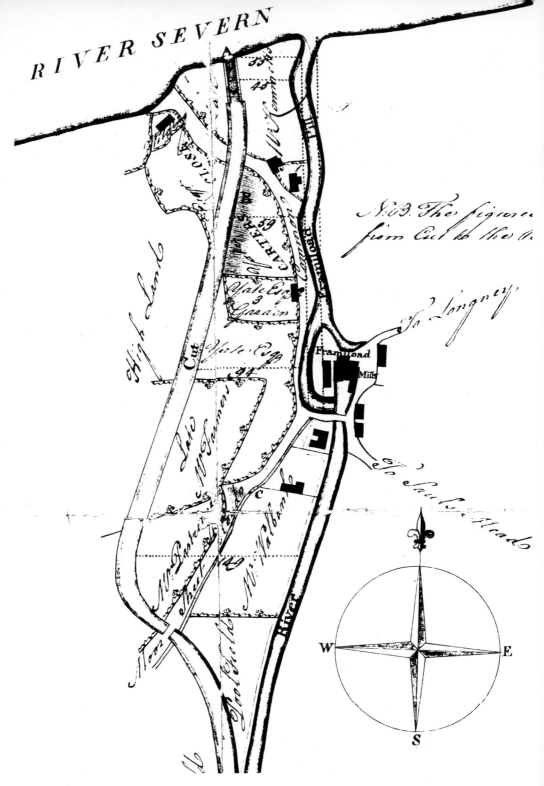

Carter's Close, Framilode

this area. Thomas Yeoman, the consulting engineer employed by the Company, stayed here during his survey in 1775 and later ships carpenters were accommodated while the gates for Framilode Lock were being constructed. The Company paid their bill – an unusual step for any canal company and probably indicative of the difficulty they may have had finding suitable carpenters for the first canal in the county. After the Company Chairman, William Dallaway, had laid the first stone on 30 May 1775 the directors and many of the neighbouring gentlemen dined together at Mr. Hall's under an awning specially erected for the occasion. These and other early extravagances were regretted later when the Company ran short of money with the canal still unfinished.

Village legend reports that an outside skittle alley remains underneath the gardens in front of Fromeside and, at the other end of the building, there is some evidence of a smelting works in the gardens at the side and rear of The Cottage. Some years ago when the cesspit was built a token to pay mariners was discovered. This was subsequently given to relatives in Gloucester. Evidence of its whereabouts would be appreciated. The New Inn evidently passed into Company ownership at some stage and was used as a grace and favour home for retired lock keepers for many years. Both parts of the building were sold by the Canal Company after the last war.

Continuing along the road with the River Frome and Framilode Pill coming closer on your left you will see a new detached house on the same side just before the river bridge. This area between the road and the river here is known as the Pound, and until a few years ago formed an island between two arms of the Frome. Standing on the river bridge and looking downstream it is just possible to discern the brick foundations of Framilode Mill built at right angles across the line of the Frome to take advantage of the water power generated by the river flow. The Mill is clearly marked on the plan of Carter's Close shown opposite and stood on the river a few yards below the site of the modern house. The mill race, also shown on the plan, left the Frome immediately below the river bridge on your left ran behind the telephone box, kept within a few inches of the road and rejoined the main river just below the house.

This area is significant for the Stroudwater Canal since the line of the Frome from the Severn a hundred yards or so away, the mill race round the mill, and the line of the Frome behind you above the bridge mark the line of both Richard Owen Cambridge's private canal built in the 1740s, and John Kemmett's highly original Canal of 1759-63 built with cranes instead of locks to effect the change in levels. The crane at Framilode Mill, positioned where the mill race left the Frome just below the bridge, lifted container boxes out of small craft on the lower level and transferred them to separate craft running on the higher pound. The layout of this is shown in the plan here.

which carried coal from Bullo Pill on the Forest of Dean side of the Severn. Purcell unloaded a regular cargo at Framilode and then distributed it by lorry to his customers in the Saul area until the mid 1930s. Eventually, when the ageing *Rose* became unsafe, he tied her up at the small winding hole on the offside just above Framilode swing bridge. The *Rose* was later sold to Charlie Camm who took her out into the river and used her as a sunken breakwater to prevent his land being eroded by the Severn. This passage of the *Rose* through Framilode Lock in the late 1930s is the last recorded use of the lock.

Continuing along the towpath you will pass half a dozen or so more houses which also face away from the canal even though most of them, like Canal Row and other houses in Framilode, were occupied by mariners and boat men in the late eighteenth and nineteenth centuries. The wall on your left just as the canal curves leftwards hides the former Cookley's Wharf. Mr. Cookley unloaded his coal boat at his wharf here just before Moor Street bridge until the late 1930s. The renovated building just before the bridge was originally boat men's stables and a blacksmith's shop. This was the last regular traffic down this length of canal below Saul Junction. These craft were long boats from the Stafford area carrying thirty tons or so at a time, not the earlier broad-beamed Stroudwater barges and Severn trows which carried coal from riverside ports like Bullo Pill and Lydney. The long boats came down the Severn, along the Gloucester and Berkeley Canal and locked down into the Stroudwater Canal at Junction Lock, Saul. They winded in Framilode Basin and returned to Saul Junction. Cookley distributed the coal using a horse and cart.

Crossing Moor Street bridge, which was originally a swing bridge, the towpath continues for a hundred yards or so before terminating where the Frome has been widened and the bed of the canal used as part of the flood relief channel. The lands to the left and right on this short stretch were part of Pool Field when the canal was built. It was poor land, ill-drained and still used as strip fields in 1776 when part was used as a brick yard when the canal was built. The banks in Pool Fields gave the Canal Company trouble from the early days and leaks remain a problem in this area.

At this point it is as well to stop for a few moments and consider the significance of the hamlet we have seen. It is one of very few towns or villages created to serve the needs of an expanding waterborne trade – first the river and later the canal. It is therefore of comparable significance to the canal village of Shardlow on the Trent and Mersey Canal in Derbyshire and Stourport at the junction of the Staffordshire and Worcestershire Canal and the River Severn. Both these settlements are designated Conservation Areas. In addition a Derbyshire Historical Buildings Trust, originally financed by the County Council but now self-supporting, has created a revolving fund to buy houses of historic interest similar to the canalside buildings at Framilode, renovate them carefully and sensitively and then resell the properties at a profit using the surplus created each time to widen the activities of the Trust. A thoughtful county council would consider making Framilode a conservation area and any local amenity society worth its salt would work with them, the Civic Trust, and other county based groups like the Cottage Improvement Societies to create a similar Gloucestershire Historical Buildings Trust which might also become self supporting. New, well-planned modern infill settlement – especially if it were designed with an eye on existing canal structures and layout – might even enhance a village like this. As it is too many villages and towns of historic interest all over the country are threatened with unsuitable styled modern housing, with garish and obtrusive brickwork which detracts rather than adds to the amenities of the area.

The River Frome, Cambridge Canal, Kemmett Canal and Stroudwater Canal all run together now the flood prevention scheme of the mid 1970s has merged them into one broad channel. Plate Nineteen of *The Stroudwater Canal* gives some idea of the former relationship between the canal and river here. The Frome itself was probably straightened along this length as part of the Cambridge or Kemmett improvements sometime between the mid 1740s and early 1760s.

Although the river bank here is private property, and there are no stiles through the fences, the owners have kindly given me permission to direct people to follow the line of the canal by walking along the right hand bank of the river as far as the Junction at Saul. Please climb over the wooden fences carefully and keep any dogs with you on a lead.

The last craft to use this length of canal below the Junction was the Stroudwater barge *Stanley* whose remains are shown on Plate Twenty of *The Stroudwater Canal* where it is wrongly referred to as a Severn trow. It was left in this disused section of canal in the early 1940s after carrying the last cargo from Bullo Pill and up the Gloucester and Berkeley Canal to Stroud Gas Works – a journey it made regularly for many years. The *Stanley* lost its superstructure first and then sank soon afterwards. It was finally broken up when the new flood prevention works were built.

There are no features of any interest on this length for three quarters of a mile or so until you approach a long house on your right which stands on the former banks of the canal at an angle to the line of the navigation. Now a private house, this is reputed to have been built around the 1780s as three cottages and used as homes by boatmen's families. The building also included a bakery. It was taken over by Stroud Brewery at some time late in the eighteenth century and converted into a public house called the Drum and Monkey. It was common for boat men to tie up here and use the public house. Sometime

37

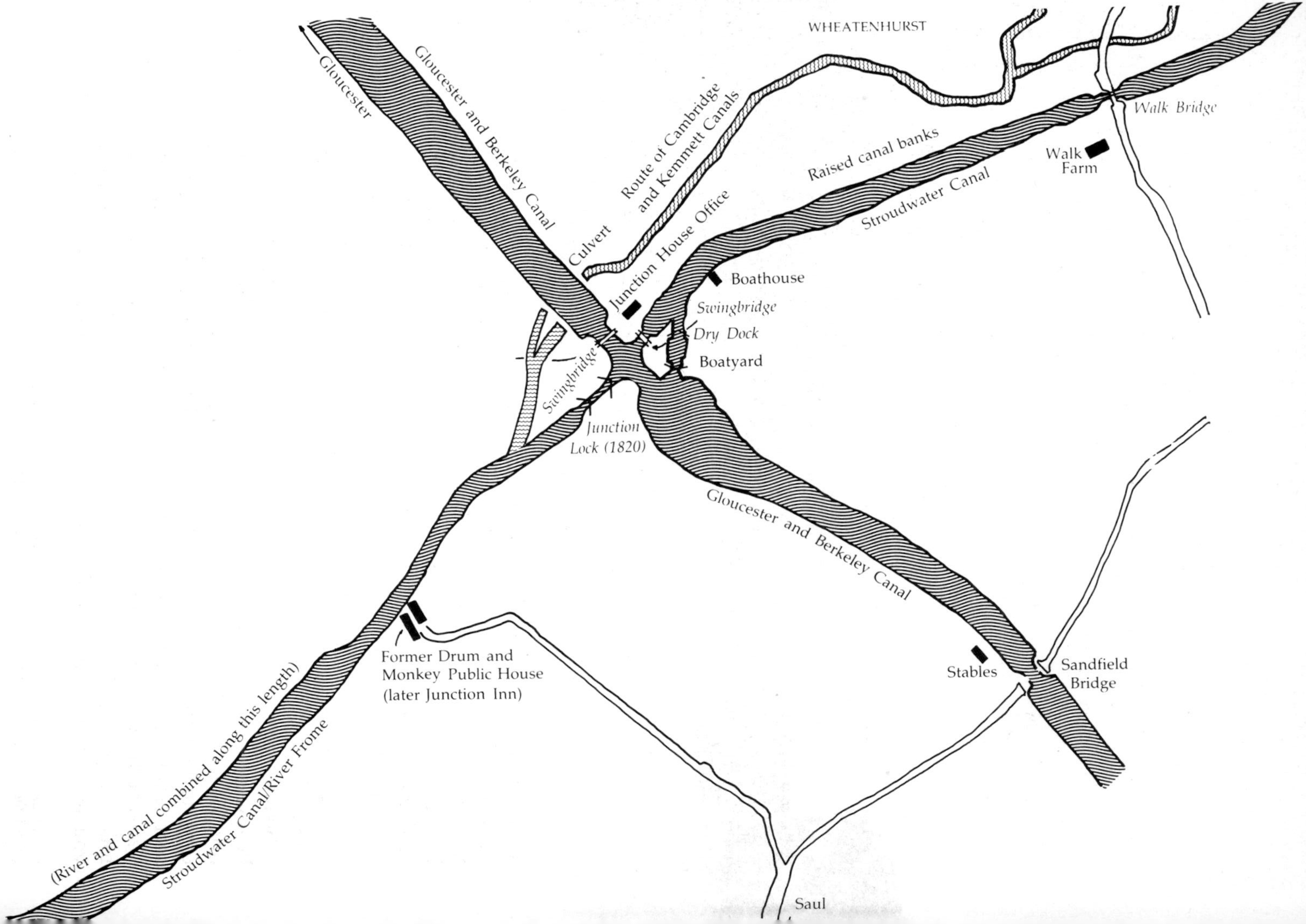

WHEATENHURST

Walk Bridge

Walk Farm

Raised canal banks

Stroudwater Canal

Route of Cambridge and Kennet Canals

Junction House Office

Culvert

Boathouse

Swingbridge
Dry Dock
Boatyard

Swingbridge

Junction Lock (1820)

Gloucester and Berkeley Canal

Gloucester

Gloucester

Sandfield Bridge

Stables

Saul

Gloucester and Berkeley Canal

Former Drum and Monkey Public House (later Junction Inn)

Stroudwater Canal/River Frome
(River and canal combined along this length)

after the Gloucester and Berkeley Canal was built to Saul in 1820 the name was changed to the Junction Inn and boat men from the ship canal frequented it as well. Charles Oakley Lawrence was the last landlord before the house returned to private ownership in 1968. A few yards further on there is another dwelling, parallel to the former public house. This was originally three cottages called Junction Cottages, but has been converted to one private house in recent years. Here again there are suggestions the houses were frequently tenanted by boatmen and their families when the canal was in its heyday.

Standing parallel to the line of the canal a little further on is the small boathouse where 'Grampy' Warren built light craft within living memory. At this point the Frome and the Stroudwater Canal diverge. The canal turns a little to the right and runs up to Junction Lock which is best seen from the Junction towpath rather than following the Stroudwater Canal at this point. Keep on top of the floodbank of the River Frome and follow the path to the left of the concrete Wycliffe College boathouse and you will emerge onto the Gloucester and Berkeley Canal towpath.

4. Saul Junction date unknown. Junction Lock is visible on the left. The canal crossed the Berkeley Canal here in front of Junction House.

CHAPTER THREE

Saul Junction to Bristol Road

When you emerge onto the Gloucester and Berkeley Canal towpath it is a good idea to stand still for a few minutes to take in the general features of the scene around you before moving on to the junction to examine those features in greater detail. The large ship canal in front of you was started in 1794 when commercial traffic on inland and tidal waterways was an important factor in the local economy. The original Act was passed during the 'Canal Mania' of 1793 and after several false starts with financial crises, constructional difficulties and disputes with both contractor and engineers, the canal was extended as far as this junction with the Stroudwater Canal at Saul in 1820. The plan to link with the Severn at Berkeley Pill was amended to save money and the canal was completed to Sharpness in 1827. For this reason it is now sometimes referred to as the Gloucester and Sharpness Canal although many local and canal-minded people still prefer to call it 'The Berkeley Canal'.

The River Severn below the port of Gloucester has never been a safe waterway for any type of craft. The constantly changing sandbanks, the wide variation in flow, the sudden winds, the beds of rock crossing the channel at various points, the rapid floods, the huge tidal range and the famous Severn Bore have all taken their toll of craft over the centuries. The *Gloucester Journal* is littered with the records of missing passage boats and lost cargoes on this unpredictable river. The construction of the Gloucester and Berkeley Canal provided a safe alternative to the Severn route. The canal has had a long history of mixed fortunes. It was always a busy commercial waterway and this volume of traffic led to the canal being widened and deepened a number of times. It remains one of the British Waterways Board's most important commercial waterways and there are good prospects of further change in the 1980s linked with the development of the Severn as a major waterway. Current assessments for the proposed Severn Barrage Scheme continue to improve and this could also have a major impact on the future of Lower Severnside. Financially, the Gloucester and Berekeley Canal had large outstanding debts in its early years. Although it left a legacy of outstanding industrial buildings at Gloucester Docks it failed to achieve one major objective of its promoters – turning Gloucester into an important national port.

The Gloucester and Berkeley Canal was opened to Saul Junction in

1820 though a permanent connection was not completed until 1826. This new route reduced the significance of the section of Stroudwater Canal running down to the Severn at Framilode. The Stroudwater itself was built specifically to accommodate Severn trows carrying coal from the Midlands to Stroud, although the lock sizes were incidentally large enough to take two long boats. Coal cargoes from Shropshire therefore usually travelled down the Severn in trows to Framilode Lock and entered the Stroudwater Canal there. Similarly coal cargoes from Staffordshire or Worcestershire were carried down the canals to the Severn at Stourport or Worcester and then transhipped there into trows for the final part of their journey down the Severn and into the Stroudwater Canal at Framilode. This transhipment was essential since the tidal Severn below Gloucester had never been safe for loaded canal boats with only a few inches of freeboard.

The new ship canal allowed Shropshire trows to travel down the Severn, lock into non-tidal water at Gloucester and take the direct route to the Stroudwater Canal at Saul rather than the indirect route via Framilode. It also abolished the need for transhipment at Stourport or Worcester since canal boats could now travel the same route just as safely. A similar pattern developed for the much smaller volume of mixed cargoes coming up the Severn when the Berkeley Canal was opened from Saul to Sharpness. Trows entered the ship canal at Sharpness and joined the Stroudwater Canal at Saul without any need to use the lock at Framilode. The Framilode to Saul section of the Stroudwater Canal therefore became obsolete for any Stroud bound cargoes coming any distance up or down the Severn.

However, for many years the main traffic using the Stroudwater Canal consisted of coal coming across the Severn from Bullo Pill, and other small riverside ports on the Forest side of the river. All these cargoes used the Framilode entrance to the Canal. When the relative importance of coal from the Forest of Dean declined in the nineteenth century, and that from Midland sources came to dominate the Stroudwater trade, the significance of the Saul to Framilode pound was reduced still further. The Stroudwater, Thames & Severn Canal Trust have no plans at present to restore this pound as part of their plans for reopening the two canals to the Thames. It seems sad to reflect this section of canal may now be lost for ever. Perhaps we need an organisation for canals similar to that organised by the Friends of Friendless Churches. This short pound to the Severn would be a prime candidate for its early attention. The Severn Barrage Scheme would greatly increase the amenity potential of the river and increase the need for a restored section from Framilode to Saul. But by then it may be too late.

Saul Junction is an interesting area. The graceless boathouse behind you to your right belongs to Wycliffe College. It is used for storing boats for the school rowing crews. The College has an earlier boathouse standing adjacent to the Stroudwater Canal in the school grounds at Stonehouse, but this was replaced by the boathouse at Saul when the canal at Stonehouse became disused.

The weir to your left acts as an overflow from the Gloucester and Berkeley Canal to the River Frome which flows under the ship canal at this point. It stands on the site of the original line of the Stroudwater Canal built in 1775-9 which was altered when the new ship canal formed a junction with the older canal in 1820. The relationship between the earlier and present pattern of routes is clear from the map on page 303 of Charles Hadfield's *Canals of South and South East England* which is reproduced here with his permission. There were no locks on the Stroudwater Canal between Framilode and Whitminster, so the original level of the canal in this area was the same as that on the Framilode pound. Since both canal companies wanted the two canals to meet on

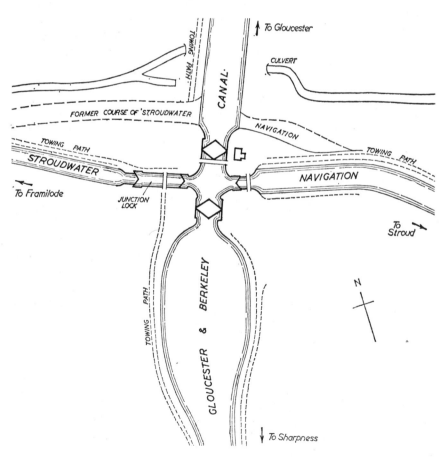

one level it was necessary to install an additional lock on the Stroudwater Canal, now called Junction Lock, and to raise the level of the pound
on a slight embankment from the junction to the tail of Whitminster
Lock. Apart from the new line of the Stroudwater Canal at the junction,
the improved line followed exactly the same route as the old canal. The
new and old Stroudwater lines joined up together about a hundred
yards below the junction and about the same distance above the
junction where the Stroudwater Canal turns right slightly as it
approaches the long straight to Walk Bridge at Whitminster. There are
no remains of the old line below this point at the junction now, but if
you look across the ship canal you can perhaps see how the land dips
down behind Junction Bridge House. The old Stroudwater line ran
roughly halfway between the Frome and Junction Bridge House.

Turning to your right now, and walking past the College boathouse
you will come to the junction of the two canals. All the changes here –
the new lock, the new section of canal and the raised banks – were
installed and paid for by the Gloucester and Berkeley Canal Company
when the junction was made. Junction Lock itself is a good example of
this and the way in which different canal companies developed different
designs which show right down to the present day. The lock is built of
stone whereas most Stroudwater locks are built of brick. The design of
the gates, the type of balance beam and the style of the paddle gear all
mark it out as different from the usual Stroudwater pattern. These
differences reflect the fact that the lock was maintained by the Gloucester and Berkeley Canal Company and their successors the British
Waterways Board as part of the agreement with the Company of
Proprietors of the Stroudwater Navigation made when the new junction
was planned. The swing bridge across the lock is now fixed shut though
the lock itself would make a useful dry dock if it was fully repaired. The
new junction here was specifically designed and executed to minimise
interference with regular Stroudwater traffic during construction.

Turning round now and looking across the junction once again you
get a good view of a number of interesting features. From the left you
will see first the large swing footbridge across the Gloucester and
Berkeley Canal. This bridge is so finely balanced that the bridgekeeper
can move this substantial structure with a minimum of effort. Notice the
traffic lights to control commercial traffic on the main canal at this
constricted part of the navigation. The present bridgekeeper is Harold
Brown who lives in the attractive house at the junction known as
Junction Bridge House. This interesting Georgian building stands facing
the Stroudwater Canal and is similar to the lockhouse at Framilode as
well as other houses with canal connections at Chippenham Platt,
Newtown and Ryeford Double Locks. Nevertheless this too was built by
the Gloucester and Berkeley Canal Company around 1820 and has

always been maintained by the Gloucester and Berkeley Canal owners rather than the Stroudwater proprietors.

The smaller iron swingbridge across the entrance to the Stroudwater Canal opposite the point you are standing was installed around 1886 by the Stroudwater Company at the same time other iron swing-bridges were installed at Framilode and elswehere. Their constructional profile is interesting. Each bridge has a thick vertical iron bar located near the pivotal position. The section of the bridge which swings across the canal is supported by iron suspension bars running from the vertical bar to the base of the bridge. The smaller type of iron swing bridge like the one at the junction here had two suspension bars running in each direction while the larger ones such as at Ebley Cloth Mills bridge had four suspension bars running in each direction. Originally these bridges all had iron handles to assist opening and closing, but this has been replaced at Saul. Each of these late-nineteenth-century iron swing bridges superseded earlier wooden swing bridges on the canal which needed replacement after almost a hundred years of constant use.

Beneath the swing bridge you will notice the stop gates which were installed at the same time as the other works at the junction. The small flat roofed building to the right of the bridge is a former BWB office built in the forgettable style known as '1950s Municipal'. It is now used as an office for the boatyard and sadly shows no sign of imminent collapse. The modern British Waterways Board has won several major conservation awards in recent years as a result of the outstanding work of its architect Peter White. It is unlikely that such a banal design for such an attractive area would nowadays pass the critical eyes of his imaginative team.

Take the path across the large swing bridge noticing the two sets of stop gates beneath the bridge. These enable the ship canal to be drained either side of the bridge for repairs and maintenance. Turning right at the end of the bridge, walk up the line of the Stroudwater Canal to get a closer look at the smaller iron swing bridge over the smaller set of stop gates on the older canal. Even though several of the other Stroudwater swing bridges installed at the same time had dates stamped on them – the Framilode one had '1886' on it for example – I have not been able to discover a date on this bridge. I will always be pleased to receive any further information on this as well as any other suggestions and/or corrections for future editions of this towpath guide. Keep your eyes open, too, for a new notice board at the junction area which the Stroudwater, Thames and Severn Canal Trust are planning to install to provide up to date information about the restoration of the two canals.

It is well worth stopping to have a brief chat with the bridgekeeper, Harold Brown, if he is not too busy. You will find him friendly, approachable and only too willing to share his knowledge of the junction area with you. His small office is located at the side of Junction Bridge House a few yards up the canal. Harold can often tell you when the next commercial traffic is expected up the Berkeley Canal and if you feel like waiting to see this – and even if you do not – I can recommend his tea garden at the rear of Junction Bridge House where you can relax with tea and tasty sandwiches at a very moderate cost. If it is colder weather Harold may often invite you to share his office fire and have your tea with him. British Waterways are fortunate to find someone like Harold with such an obvious interest in his job, a love of the area and a gift of sharing his interests with visitors.

One additional advantage of stopping for refreshment here is that you can get a closer look at the Cambridge and Kemmett lines as well as the route of the original Stroudwater Canal at the junction. These all run through the garden at the rear of Junction Bridge House. From the garden you can see the River Frome running up to Whitminster House in the distance to your right. This river was the route of both Richard Owen Cambridge's Canal and the later Kemmett Canal. Richard Owen Cambridge lived at Whitminster House and owned a great deal of the surrounding area. The original line of the Stroudwater Canal before the Gloucester and Berkeley Canal was built is just visible here too. It runs between the Frome and Junction Bridge House and forms a slight dip halfway down the lawn running parallel to the river. Looking at the peaceful garden today it seems difficult to believe it hides the remains of three earlier canals running up this part of the valley.

Please do not walk up the line of the River Frome beyond the garden area. This forms part of the private grounds of Whitminster House, and in any case the river runs very close to the next part of the towpath walk for half a mile or so and can be seen to greater advantage from there.

Opposite Junction Bridge House there is a busy dry dock and boatyard, building and repairing both pleasure and commercial craft. A small brick built boathouse with granite block foundations faces the Stroudwater Canal on the offside a few yards away. This may be one of several known pleasure boathouses built on the canal in the early to mid nineteenth century. A smaller more recent boathouse is visible on Plate 31 of *The Stroudwater Canal* and there was another at Wallbridge where the Company pleasure barge was kept. There was a crane on the bank to the left of the boathouse at the junction but this has now disappeared. This area was the site of Walter Clark's coal wharf in the late nineteenth and early twentieth centuries. It must have been a lucrative trade since he owned several properties in Framilode at the time.

Walking up the Stroudwater Canal you will notice how it turns slightly to the right a few yards further on. It was at this point on the towpath side that the original line of the canal rejoined the modern Stroudwater line. From here to Whitminster Lock the original and later

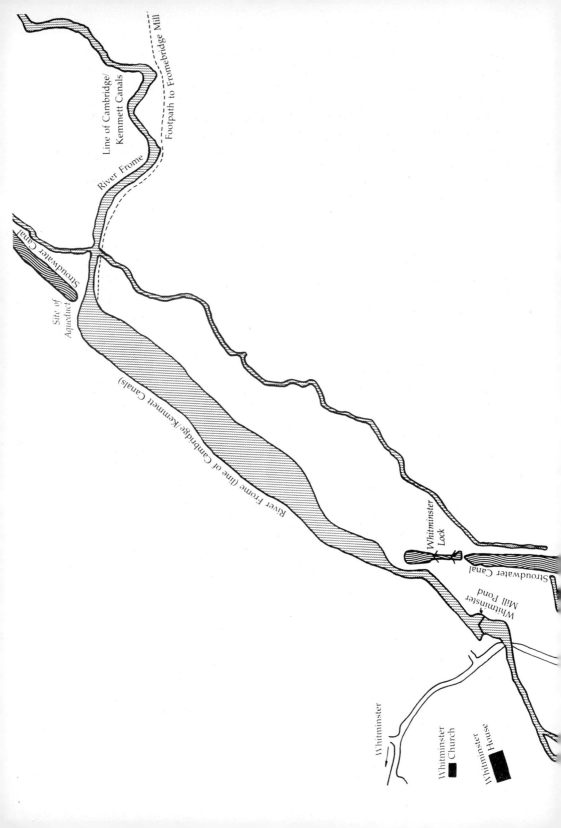

lines cover the same ground though the original line was at a much lower level as far as the tail of Whitminster Lock. The post-1820 Stroudwater Canal was embanked above the surrounding land here to bring it up to the level of the ship canal.

The section of canal as far as Whitminster Lock was bought by the British Transport Commission (Waterways) in 1954 as part of the closure agreement negotiated with the Stroudwater proprietors. The BTC purchased this length to guarantee their control of the Frome water intake near Whitminster Lock which supplies this pound of the Stroudwater Canal and hence the Gloucester and Berkeley Canal as well. The sale was a short-sighted error of judgement by the older canal company. It now forms one of the most lucrative BWB moorings in the country and is listed in their 'Special' price class.

As you head towards Walk Bridge you will see the Cambridge/Kemmett line of the Frome on your left and get a good view of Cambridge's former residence at Whitminster House now owned by Major John Teesdale. Approaching Walk Bridge you will notice on your left that the Frome here divides into two separate channels. One of these, known to be an early line of the river, continues to run parallel to the canal. The other turns and runs broadly at right angles to the canal in the general direction of Whitminster House. This second channel forms part of the mill race of the former Whitminster Mill situated nearby and was the route used by Cambridge and Kemmett for their own canals. It was altered as part of a Severn-Trent Authority flood prevention scheme in the mid 1970s.

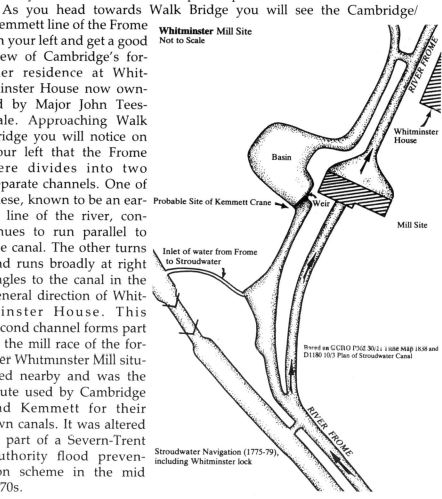

Whitminster Mill Site
Not to Scale

River Frome

Whitminster House

Basin

Probable Site of Kemmett Crane ➤ Weir

Mill Site

Inlet of water from Frome to Stroudwater

Based on GCRO P362 30/21 Tithe Map 1838 and D1180 10/3 Plan of Stroudwater Canal

River Frome

Stroudwater Navigation (1775–79), including Whitminster lock

47

Walk Bridge was originally a wooden swing bridge. It is now a fixed structure and forms the first major obstacle to restoration on the Stroud side of the junction. The consulting engineers to the canal trust, Freeman Fox and Partners, produced a preliminary report in August 1976 on the feasibility of restoring the two canals to through navigation. They recommend that either a new fixed bridge with 6'6" headroom should be constructed here or, perhaps more sensibly, a substantially built lift bridge capable of carrying buses and the heavy lorry traffic which use this road.

Looking across the other side of Walk Bridge and up the canal you can see once again the embanked nature of this section of canal as far as the tail of the Whitminster Lock site. Turn left up the road towards Whitminster House. Almost at once you will see a pathway going off through a gate on your left. Walk up here a few yards and over the first culvert. This small stream is the same early line of the Frome we saw approaching Walk Bridge on the canal. Continue along this path until you approach a second small bridge about a hundred yards further on. Go towards the farm gate or smaller gate on your left just before you reach this bridge and look towards the river. The stream coming in from your right is a new flood relief channel installed by the Severn Trent Water Authority in the mid 1970s. The other stream which is running towards you and joins the flood relief channel at right angles in front of where you are standing is the line of the Cambridge and Kemmett Canals. Here, where the mill race stream was brought as close to Whitminster House as possible, Richard Owen Cambridge built a small wharf to land stone and building materials for his estate. This was the place where Frederick Louis, Prince of Wales, and his party alighted when they spent a day on Cambridge's private canal in 1750. It is tempting to wonder whether the wooden piles and ironwork which are visible on the Cambridge/Kemmett line date from this period. Just out of your view the early canal line turns sharp right and runs more or less straight in the direction of Whitminster weir.

Retrace your steps to the path, turn towards Whitminster House and walk on for a few yards over the flood relief channel. Within a few more steps you will come to the Cambridge/Kemmett line again where you can see the route running down to the wharf corner and upstream towards the former site of Whitminster Mill. Notice the remains of wooden piles now in the bed of the canal below the bridge. The flood relief channel now carries the bulk of Frome water not taken by the Gloucester and Berkeley Canal intake nearby. The volume of water which runs along the Cambridge/Kemmett line is therefore very much less than in Richard Owen Cambridge's day. This partly explains why the line itself is very much narrower and shallower than it must have been around 1750. If we appreciate this change it makes it easier to understand how Cambridge's small man-towed craft could have used this unlikely looking stretch of waterway.

Please do not go any further into the Whitminster estate than this bridge or take the short cut in front of the house to Whitminster weir. We hope to be able to continue the generous access which Major Teesdale has allowed to the old Cambridge/Kemmett Canals. Your responsible behaviour in these private grounds will be a great help to future generations of visitors.

Retrace your steps towards the Walk Bridge turning left up the lane as soon as you reach the road. Once again you will pass over the original line of the Frome and, after a hundred yards or so, come to the bridge over the modern line of the Frome. This length of river was originally built as the mill race for Whitminster Mill, was incorporated in both the Cambridge and Kemmett Canals and is now utilised as part of the main route of the River Frome. Turning round and looking upstream you will see Whitminster weir. Whitminster Mill stood on the left here roughly where the modern bungalow is situated. The Kemmett crane would be positioned somewhere on the right hand side of the weir here so that it could lift the container boxes from the lower to the upper level without interfering with the work of the mill.

From Walk Bridge, walk up the left hand bank of the embanked Stroudwater Canal. The original line of the River Frome – now reduced to a trickle – is on your left and this passes underneath the canal as you approach the remains of Whitminster Lock. The iron-swing bridge topped with concrete here is now fixed and the lock itself has been filled in. When it was completed in 1776, Whitminster Lock had a fall of about four feet, but this was reduced to only a few inches when the Gloucester and Berkeley Canal was opened. Between the old swing bridge and the Frome you will see the large water intake from the river into the ship canal. This reduces the flow of the Frome below the intake to only a small proportion of its former flow.

The towpath of the Stroudwater Canal crosses over the canal at this point so you should cross over the site of the swing bridge and keep the canal on your left. From Whitminster Lock for a distance of about six hundred yards or so the canal has been incorporated into the river to form one wide channel sufficient to take excess flood water. The original Stroudwater Canal used the river bed between Whitminster Lock and Lockham Bridge but this was found to be unsatisfactory as river silt interfered with the passage of trows. Within a few years the river and canal were separated and remained so until the 1970s flood prevention scheme. The canal line ran to the left of the bank on which you are walking and the river ran in a separate channel a few yards further to the left. This narrow bank of land between the canal and river was removed when the two channels were amalgamated. The length of river here as far as the site of the former aqueduct at Lockham Bridge was part of the mill pond feeding the waterwheel at Whitminster Mill.

Follow the towpath until you come to a small riverside wood. It is easiest here to walk around this woodland and rejoin the towpath about a hundred yards or so further on. Where the Frome and canal separate once again climb over the double stile, over the new footbridge across the Frome and rejoin the line of the canal a short distance further on. This modern footbridge stands on the site of a much earlier river bridge called Lockham Bridge which existed before the canal was built. When the canal was built an aqueduct carried the navigation over the river. This was demolished when the flood relief scheme merged canal & river routes here in the 1970s.

This place where the river and canal separate is significant since it marks the last time the older Cambridge/Kemmett Canals and the river Stroudwater Canal came together. The older canals followed the line of the river from here to Bristol Road where the Cambridge Canal terminated. The Kemmett Canal continued to Stonehouse. The best way to see all these canals on one visit is to walk along the Stroudwater Canal to Bristol Road, retrace your steps to this junction and then walk up the left hand bank of the Cambridge/Kemmett Canal as far as Fromebridge Mill on the A38.

Rejoining the Stroudwater Canal near Lockham Bridge you can either turn left for a hundred yards or so past the concrete pill box installed during the Second World War to where the canal is stanked off or omit this short section of canal altogether and turn right along the canal towards Bristol Road. The towing path is wide along this stretch and you can see plenty of evidence of dredgings which have accumulated over the years. Notice, too, near a second pill box a small weir running underneath the towpath which can be used to control the level of the canal.

Stonepits Bridge was originally a swing bridge probably named from some stone pits nearby. There are gravel workings on the other side of the Frome Valley over half-a-mile away on the outskirts of Frampton-on-Severn and others near where the Frampton road joins the A38. The area known as Claypits about a mile or so away on the Bristol Road probably had a similar origin. There is a wide lane leading from Stonepits Bridge up towards Whitminster village though part of this lane near the bridge itself is now disused and a newer track runs up the hillside by the hedge to join the road near Whitminster school. Local legend suggests this land and the early Lockham Bridge were both the original route to the old Whitminster village near Whitminster House before the new road was built to the House from the top of the lane, and that route used by horse-drawn carts carrying stone from the stone pits to the Whitminster area. If this is so, and the stone pits were still being used when the canal was built, a swing bridge would be preferable for the horse drawn carts rather than the steep incline of a brick built arched bridge.

The canal runs more or less in a straight line from Lockham Bridge to Bristol Road. It is an attractive stretch with its waterlilies and abundant wildlife. The whole section is well maintained by Tuffley Angling Club and there is little of the old bread wrappings, throw-away drink cans and general untidiness which is sometimes so obvious on lengths of waterway used by less responsible anglers.

The next feature, visible from Stonepits, is a well preserved brick structure called Occupation Bridge built to provide access for a farm divided when the canal came through the parish. It is characteristic of this section of canal through the Vale of Gloucester where the building materials used reflect the underlying clay geology of the area. Notice the simplicity of the form and the way it serves its purpose without pretension. The similarity to some Midlands canal bridges reflects both the utility of the design and the way in which different engineers and clerks of works moved from one canal to another as canals were built often using the same basic patterns of construction. The Stroudwater Canal has particularly strong design similarities to the Staffordshire and Worcestershire Canal and the Droitwich Barge Canal for these reasons. Apart from some small scale repairs in a different brick the bridge is unchanged from when it was built in 1776. There is an excellent view of the canal and surrounding area from the bridge including the Cambridge/Kemmett Canals to your right. Underneath the bridge there are some striking examples of rope markings. All over the canal systems generations of tow ropes wore into the brickwork of bridges and locks. Companies such as the Stroudwater often tried to protect them with iron bars but even then the volume of traffic over the years and the constant friction etched themselves deeply into the ironwork. These rope markings serve as eloquent reminders of the sheer intensity of use our forefathers took for granted on Britain's heritage of inland waterways. Just as eloquently they stand in silent reproach to our current neglect.

There is a third pill box on the towpath side as the canal approaches the A38 and then, on the opposite side of the canal, the Bristol Road Wharf. The canal was open from Framilode to here on 17 December 1776 and the first cargo was sixty tons of coal.

There are two main buildings at Bristol Road. The house nearest the main road is Wharf House build in 1776 by John Insull and first occupied by Joseph Grazebrook, clerk to the Canal Company in January 1777. The oldest part of the house is furthest away from the canal although recent renovations suggest that even this may have been built in two halves. If this is correct, the original house was a one up, one down structure in the centre of the house. At some later date, perhaps in the early 1780s,

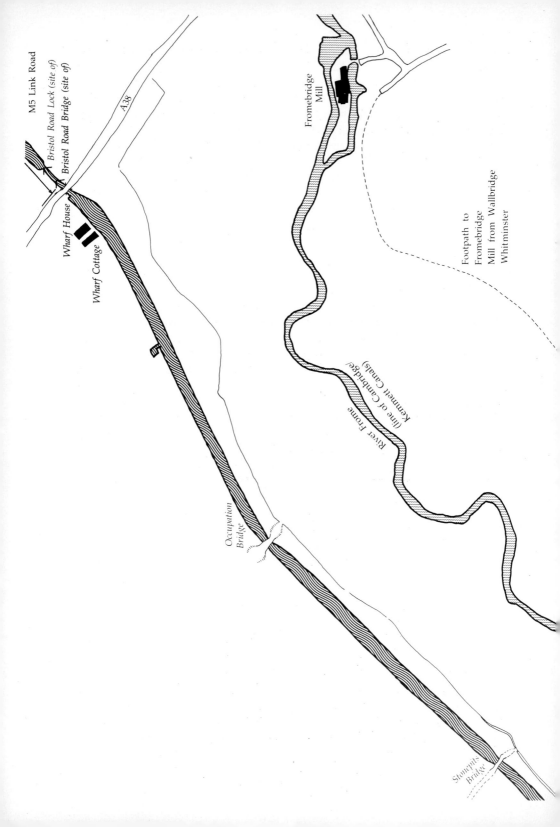

M5 Link Road

Bristol Road Lock (site of)
Bristol Road Bridge (site of)

A38

Wharf House

Wharf Cottage

Fromebridge Mill

Footpath to Fromebridge Mill from Wallbridge Whitminster

River Frome (line of Cambridge/ Kennett Canals)

Occupation Bridge

Stonepits Bridge

the house had an additional single storey building on the side furthest from the canal. Later on still, probably around 1786, this was converted into a two storey building and the original house was therefore doubled in size to a two up, two down dwelling. It looks as if the poor quality facing bricks used when the house was first built and probably made from clay dug out of the canal line were replaced about this time. The entire house was refaced with the better quality facing bricks which still survive. The history of the second building at the wharf, Wharf Cottage, remains obscure though it may have been added at about this time.

During its early life Wharf House served beer to the boat men through a window in the side of the house facing the canal. When the house was extended towards the canal during the early nineteenth century, this window became part of an inside wall. Once again it seems the extension started life as a single storey building. The different types of brick used on the earlier four roomed dwelling and the later six roomed dwelling are obvious to even the most unpractised eye.

In the nineteenth century, the part of the house furthest from the canal was used as a shop. Until March 1937 the house was occupied by the coal merchant Mr. Spiers who ran a coal-round to nearby villages using a horse and cart. From then until 1980, when the house was sold by the Canal Company, it was occupied by Mr. and Mrs. Davis at a tenancy of 8s. 4d. a week. For many years during the same period Wharf Cottage was let for 2s. 7d. a week. Wharf House was in an appalling state when it was sold, several ceilings had collapsed, part of the house was slipping into the canal, it was severely affected by damp, and much of the house could not be used.

Bristol Road was always one of the more important coal wharves on the canal as there was good road communications north and south from here for distributing coal to the surrounding villages.

The canal is blocked at Bristol Road (A38) by a new main road island installed on the site of the old Bristol Road Bridge and Lock. I recall this lock from the early 1970s. The top gates had rounded trunk balance beams and seemed in fair condition. The lock here was started at the end of 1776 and finished in late July 1777. James Bough, the Company stonemason, built the stone foundations and probably the brickwork as well. John Pashley made the original lock gates. The bridge was built by John Couch and John Hern although Edward Edge, the surveyor of masonry, found some of the mortar unsatisfactory and part of the bridge had to be taken down and rebuilt.

Since a new link road between the A38 and M5 has utilised part of the canal bed above Bristol Road restoration of the canal along the original line here is out of the question. There are really two options open to the canal trust in restoring the canal. The original option suggested by the consulting engineers proposed using a deepened River Frome from down to Whitminster and beyond.

The mill at Fromebridge has been working here for at least three hundred and forty years. John Taylor refers to it during his voyage down the Frome in 1641. When the Stroudwater Canal was under construction it belonged to John and William Purnell who were two of the Canal Company's most well known opponents. They owned the tin plate works at Framilode Mill as well as the iron and wire works here at Fromebridge. They had also been involved in the hilarious Battle of Carters Close at Framilode when the Canal Company navvies dug out the canal by day and its opponents filled it in under cover of night. The houses on the other side of the upper level were originally a terrace of cottages for mill employees but were converted into separate dwellings in the mid 1970s.

The new canal proposed by the consulting engineers would leave the lower water level near where you are standing and use the River Frome from here to the top side of the M5 bridge. The river would be divided into the existing upper level to supply the mill and the new lower level to act as navigation channel and take the canal under the A38 bridge.

Retrace your steps over the footbridge and past Mr. Stanley's house. Then turn left and walk on to the A38 a few yards further on. It is worth standing on the river bridge for a few moments looking back towards Fromebridge and trying to envisage what the consultants propose. Perhaps it is ironic that John Kemmett's long abandoned route for his machine navigation is being considered as the basis of a brand new canal for the 1980s.

CHAPTER FOUR

Bristol Road to Roving Bridge, Newtown

Take great care crossing the busy A38 at Fromebridge. Standing on the Stroud side of the road you can see John Kemmett's canal running along the present Frome line. The earlier Frome route is about fifty yards to your left running parallel to the modern river. Looking further across the valley you can see the A38 – M5 link road built over the canal above Bristol Road. Hydes Bridge, rebuilt in 1841 and which stood about a quarter of a mile above the lock, is completely obliterated.

The footpath along the Frome is along the right hand bank. Follow this for about three hundred yards. Here, on the opposite side of the river the original Frome course joins the present river. Continue along the footpath which follows the river bank. From this point the river runs more or less straight for some distance but was originally very much more windy than this. Along both sides of the river for the next mile or so you will notice about a dozen abandoned river meanders which John Kemmett cut off when he improved this section of river for his new canal in 1759-60. It can be useful to keep glancing at the old plan reproduced overleaf as you walk along this section, you can then trace the influence of this extraordinary man on the ground as far as Eastington.

A little further along there was a small stream which entered the Frome on the offside. This was fed from an overflow weir and sluice on the canal about a quarter of a mile above Hydes Bridge. There are a couple more meanders on the opposite side marked by willows before reaching the new motorway bridge. The consulting engineers report suggests a second lock here with the water level above being sufficient to carry the new navigation as far as Westfield Bridge.

On the Stroud side of the motorway bridge there is a large meander on the footpath side. The revised Kemmett line cut straight across this meander but the river reverted to its original course again here some-time after his navigation was left to decay in 1763.

The river is now approaching the site of Meadow Mill. On the off-side as you come towards the mill there is a new cut draining from the Chippenham Platt area of the canal. The consulting engineers propose to utilise this cut to carry the navigation from the River Frome back towards the original line of the Stroudwater Canal near

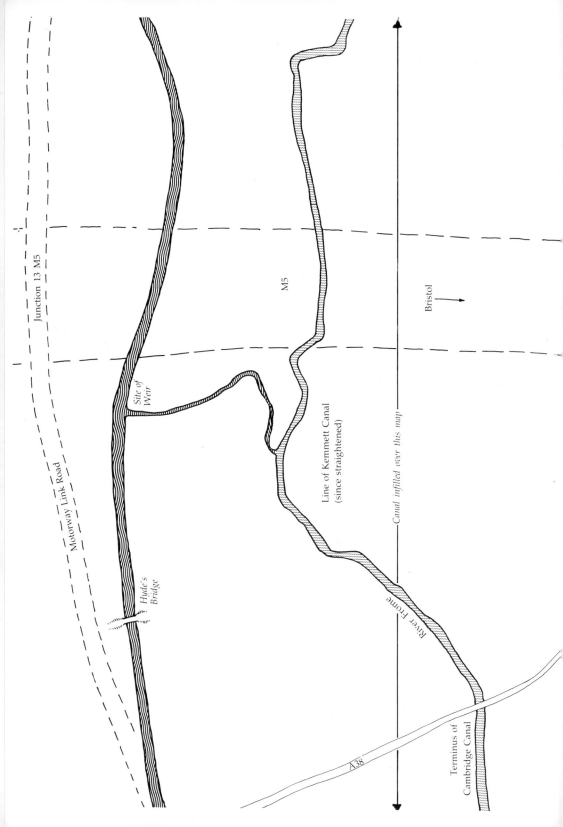

Junction 13 M5

Motorway Link Road

Site of Weir

Hyde's Bridge

M5

Line of Kemmett Canal
(since straightened)

Bristol →

River Frome

Canal infilled over this map

A38

Terminus of
Cambridge Canal

mention of additional weirs in the report but the Dadford trademark is clear enough.

Turn immediately right back onto the towing path as soon as you have crossed the stream, and walk over the small concrete bridge. Turn left and follow the fence line until you reach the site of Westfield Lock and Westfield Bridge a few yards further on.

Standing on Westfield Bridge you can look down towards the motorway and Bristol Road tracing the unfilled line of the canal in that direction. It followed closely the line of the fence on your left, past a small brick building of unknown function just below the lock, and then curved very gently to the right crossing the motorway roughly halfway between the motorway island and the Frome.

There are no remains of the canal between Westfield and Bristol Road and it is not worth considering trying to trace this section along the ground. Those of you who prefer to leave this stretch should therefore skip the next two paragraphs and start reading again at the descriptions of the Westfield Bridge area. Those who prefer to leave no stone unturned are asked to remember there is no right of way across the next half mile or so, but that the owner, Mrs. Hearsay, has kindly agreed to allow anyone to walk the original canal route *provided they close gates behind them and keep dogs under strict control*. Once again your co-operation would be appreciated. We want to keep this option open for future generations of towpath walkers and your responsible behaviour will help a great deal.

Walk across the first field and through the gate into the second field. From hereabouts the canal curved slowly away from the straight fence at the bottom of the field and followed the line of thistles towards the motorway. Use the cattle underpass to get underneath the motorway. Turn right at the other side and walk up the line of the water course parallel to the motorway for about fifty yards. If you stand back in this field and face the motorway you can see a dip in the fence which marks the route of the canal before the motorway was built. The canal then ran under the General Electric Telecommunications building and in front of the ash tree facing the two houses. It crossed the small service road and then ran straight across the fields to Bristol Road. If you walk along the A38-M5 service road stopping at the first metal gate on your left, you can see a slight hump in the new fencing about fifty yards in from the gate. The clay puddle was clearly visible here when the natural gas pipeline was being installed in 1980.

From here the canal ran in a straight line to Bristol Road gradually moving closer to the service road. It ran underneath this service road roughly where the mileage sign is situated near the A38 island.

Standing on Westfield Bridge itself you get a clear view of this line built by James Cocksey's cutting teams in the spring of 1777. You can also get a good idea of the two proposed new routes for the restored canal. The more recently suggested route would approach the bridge from about the midway point between the motorway and Chippenham Platt islands to your right. Turning around you can see the consulting engineers proposed route also coming in from your right. It would come somewhere along the line of the new channel running up from the Meadow Mill area.

If you look up the canal from Westfield Bridge you get some idea of the factors which influenced the precise route. A cursory glance at the lie of the canal ahead confirms that it did not take the obvious route of keeping close to the River Frome up the valley to Stroud. This, after all, has been the basic pattern so far. Instead the engineers built the canal up this spur of land using five locks to raise it to the long Stonehouse pound. The reason is referred to obliquely in that remarkable document written by William Dallaway and Thomas Yeoman in October 1775. The authors affirm the Canal Company had 'gone out of their way, at additional Expense, . . . to avoid cutting through the Middle of Lands, and have brought the Canal to . . . Hedge Rows, and to near Roads, wherever it was possible.' Here, at Chippenham Platt, they faced the determined opposition of the influential Ellis James. The chosen route therefore skirted James' estate at Eastington Park and took the canal up the hillside close to the turnpike road instead.

Westfield Bridge itself is not an original Stroudwater bridge. This is evident both from the 1841 date on the arch and the railway age Staffordshire blue bricks used for its construction. Canal bridges in the Vale of Gloucester were invariably built of local red brick sometimes changing to stone when the canal approached the Cotswold hills as at Dudbridge. There is a little evidence of rope marks on the bridge especially on the Stroud side.

Standing underneath the bridge you can see the blocks of stone on your right taking the towpath up to the lockside. The lock at Westfield was begun under Edmund Lingard's supervision in April 1777 and James Cocksey's team of cutters completed the canal from Bristol Road to the lock about a month later. The stream draining into the canal below Court Orchard Lock was used as a temporary feeder to fill the pound from here to Bristol Road Lock. James Bough and Edward Edge supervised the bricklayers and masons for all five locks to Eastington, and John Pashley who installed the lock gates here in October 1777 usually supplied the timberwork until he was sacked and replaced by his son Benjamin a short time afterwards.

There were mooring posts above the lock on the right-hand-side but these are no longer visible. They were used by barges, trows and long boats mooring here to unload their coal for the Meadow Mill coal pen. Returning to the coal pen, notice the steam entering the canal opposite this point. This was the temporary feeder used to fill the Bristol Road pound. The junction of the canal and feeder stream here was used as a winding hole for craft supplying the mill with coal and, on one occasion, new boilers as well. The area between the stream and the canal is known as 'the Island' or 'Potters Close'. It was used as a timber wharf for many years. There was also a boathouse on the corner of the island where canal and stream now meet.

Court Orchard is the second of five locks lifting the canal to the Stonehouse level. Like the other locks here it was started during the late summer of 1777. The building in the background is the old Wheatenhurst Union Workhouse now converted into a school. The lock name was changed when the offside area here was developed as the maintenance yard for the Stroudwater Company. This included a foreman's house known as Dock House (now The Leas), a large covered dry dock, carpenters' and blacksmiths' shops. Dock House is much altered with new windows and rendering but it retains some obvious similarities to the vernacular Georgian style of other Canal Company housing at Framilode, Bristol Road, Chippenham Platt wharf, Newtown, Ryeford and elsewhere. Notice the tooth brick course just below the roof. The house may have been built for James Bough, the Company stonemason, in 1778, and he no doubt kept an eye on both Westfield and Court Orchard Locks for his employees. There is no sign of a former lockhouse at Court Orchard Lock which probably stood on the towpath side.

The canal widens out a little at Dock House. This marks the entrance to the dry dock which stood parallel to the canal between Dock House and Court Orchard Lock. The remains of the Company icebreaker lie below the water here. The dry dock building has been demolished and the dry dock infilled, but the carpenters' shop at the back of the house and the blacksmiths' shop a little to the left are still visible from the towpath. The Company repaired all its own boats at this maintenance yard, built lock gates and swing bridges, provided ironmongery for gates etc., and used it as a store yard for timber, stone and bricks. Eventually it developed into one of the most important Canal Company installations.

There is a small overflow weir between Dock House and Eastington Wharf which drains back to the feeder stream. The wharf cottage, occupied until 1982 by one of the last traders on the canal, Mr. Leonard Beard, stands at right angles to the canal in order to keep a close watch over cargoes stored on the wharf. The cottage was probably built early in 1778 for Samuel Smith who had joined the Canal Company nearly two years earlier as foreman of a gang involved in general construction work. He was evidently a loyal and efficient employee as the Company appointed him to collect tonnages on goods landed at the wharf here.

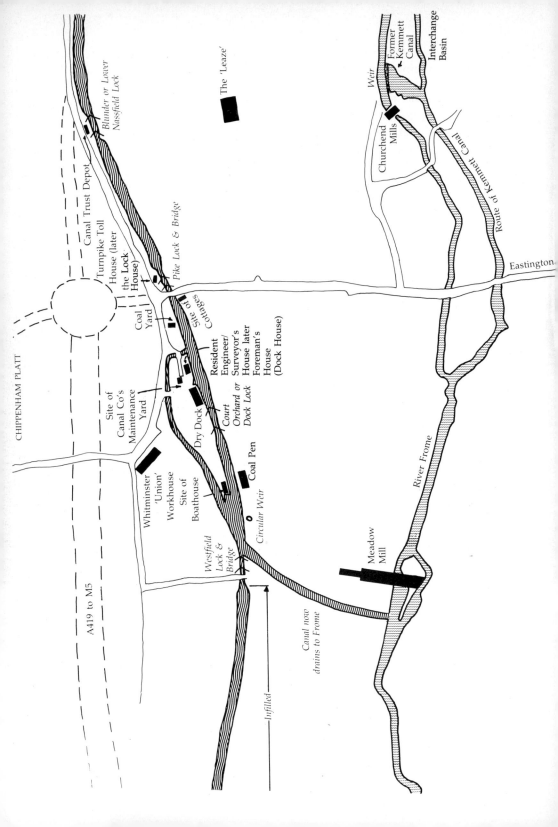

CHIPPENHAM PLATT

A419 to M5

Blunder or Lower
Nassfield Lock

Canal Trust Depot

Turnpike Toll
House (later
the Lock
House)

Pike Lock & Bridge

Coal Yard

Site of Canal Co's
Maintenance Yard

Site of
Cottages

Resident
Engineer/
Surveyor's
House later
Foreman's
House (Dock House)

Court
Orchard or
Dock Lock

Dry Dock

Coal Pen

Whitminster
'Union'
Workhouse

Site of
Boathouse

Circular Weir

Westfield
Lock &
Bridge

Infilled

Canal now
drains to Frome

The 'Leaze'

Weir

Former
Kemmett
Canal

Interchange
Basin

Churchend
Mills

Route of Kemmett Canal

Eastington

River Frome

Meadow
Mill

The wharf itself was opened on 1 January 1778 when the new carrying firm of Grazebook and Company landed twenty-five tons of lead and timber from one of their trows. For a time this became the busy and thriving head of navigation on the canal. During construction the wharf was used to store bricks, stone and timber but it was more commonly used as a coal wharf in later days. Mr. Beard says the wharf cottage was used as a cider house much frequented by boat men for many years. He bought the house and wharf from the Canal Company in 1957.

Turnpike Bridge, now more commonly called Pike Bridge, was

6. Chippenham Platt 1973. This was the site of the Company maintenance yard including carpentry and blacksmiths shops as well as the dry dock visible here.

destroyed by the county council in the 1970s. The consulting engineer to the Trust considers there is sufficient headroom to allow a bridge or box culvert to be built here although the bridge could easily be raised if required. The original Pike Bridge was replaced by an ornate bridge with a wider carriageway in the 1920s.

The towpath now changes sides once again, and keeps close to the old turnpike road. It was standard practice on all canals to build the towpath on the bank where the land fell away from the canal. This provided a wider and stronger bank on the side which was more vulnerable to landslips and leakage. The position is reversed here indicating that other factors were more influential than commonly accepted engineering techniques. Ellis James no doubt insisted the towpath should be built on the road side of the canal rather than along the edge of his estate. This minimised damage by navvies during construction and later incursions by passing boatmen and mules. Significantly the towpath reverts to the downside bank at Roving Bridge when the canal leaves the grounds of Eastington Park.

Turnpike, or more commonly Pike Lock, is a brick built structure started in July 1777 and finished almost a year later. It has been converted into an overflow weir to keep the pound above full of water. The house here was originally a toll house for the turnpike and only became a lockhouse later. The weir on the towpath side above the lock is

7. *Eastington Bridge c. 1910 showing Severn trow and Fellows, Morton and Clayton horse boat with mule or donkey towage. The cottages are now demolished but the turnpike toll house (later the lock house) still stands.*

incorporated into the domestic sewerage arrangements. This was usual practice on canals in an age before drains and sanitation. The Company mud boat was often moored on the offside here, just above the lock so the lock-keeper could keep his eye on it.

From here the canal runs through an attractive wooded stretch for about a mile or so. The belt of trees on the offside may originally have been planted on the insistence of Ellis James. This section of canal from Pike Lock to Ryeford Double Lock is being renovated by the Stroudwater, Thames & Severn Canal Trust with funds provided by the Company of Proprietors of the Stroudwater Navigation.

The next lock was originally called Lower Nassfield Lock. The Company records provide some interesting insights into the methods of canal construction. The consulting engineer, Thomas Yeoman, seems to have fixed the general route of the canal including the line up this spur of land to avoid Ellis James' lands. The precise line, including the number of locks and the rise of each, was left to the resident engineer. Edmund Lingard, for example, planned three locks above Pike Bridge with a substantial rise at Pike Lock, and smaller rises at Lower and Upper Nassfield Locks. His successor, Thomas Dadford Junior, preferred two deep locks at Pike and Upper Nassfield. Thomas Frewin, who replaced Dadford within a month, reverted to Lingard's plan for three locks with raises of 11' at Pike, 7' at Lower Nassfield and 8' at Upper Nassfield.

Edmund Lingard was one of five resident engineers employed by the Company between January 1775 and August 1779. The others included Samuel Jones, John Priddey, Thomas Frewin and Benjamin Grazebrook. The rapid turnover of skilled men suggests the Canal Company were unusually exacting and exasperating employers. This position was aggravated by two failings common on many canals. Firstly, there was the failure to agree on a specific division of responsibilities between directors and resident engineers. This often led to the committee interfering in day to day decisions not properly their concern and certainly not within their competence. Secondly inadequate costings, indifferent supervision, changes in plan and escalating costs plagued many canals including the Stroudwater. In these circumstances it is hardly surprising the committees looked round for scapegoats and that experienced engineers bitterly resented the constant harrassment.

There is ample evidence that relations between Lingard and the Canal Company deteriorated seriously in the autumn of 1777 before he was dismissed on 5 November. While it is possible that he may have excavated Lower Nassfield Lock on the wrong level by accident – Dadford's report on the construction soon after Lingard left is hardly the most flattering of documents – the fact Lingard was already under notice when the lock was started suggests strongly that he deliberately began

the lock in this way to teach a busy-bodying, self-opinionated Company a lesson they would never forget. The Company had already spent most of its original £20,000 capital by this stage and the canal was less than half completed. It could have been – and was probably intended to be – a mortal blow.

Once the news was public property it evidently provoked general merriment among the navvies and general contractors who had no doubt suffered from this regular interference too, and sympathised with Lingard's desire for some devastating revenge. Some canalside wit immediately dubbed it 'Blunder Lock' and the name passed quickly into the local vernacular. It was eventually accepted by the Company and has gone under this title ever since.

Blunder Lock was rebuilt soon afterwards using local stone instead of the standard local red brick. This may have been caused by a temporary shortage of brick supplies during construction or perhaps simply a surplus of stone left over near the lock site. There is another interesting overflow weir above the locks.

The canal continues to run close to the road. As you approach the next lock, notice the iron bar running along the edge of the stone work just below the bottom gates. This was installed both to protect the stone work from the constant wear and tear of ropes and to prevent the ropes

68

8. Chippenham Platt coal wharf date unknown. Captain and Mrs. Stephen Chandler on 'Nellie', a newly constructed de luxe Joey boat owned by white-bearded Mr. Zacharia Whiting, the village coal merchant standing on the wharf with a friend. 'Nellie' carried best quality house coal from Staffordshire via the Severn and the Berkeley Canal.

catching in the joints between the stones. Originally called Upper Nassfield Lock, this lock has simply been called Nassfield Lock since Blunder Lock was renamed in 1778, although boatmen invariably called it Top Lock of Five. Occasionally it has been incorrectly called Newtown Lock because of its nearness to the canalside hamlet of Newtown. However this name was never used by the boatmen or the Canal Company and seems to have originated with some nineteenth-century map maker with little knowledge of the canal. Today it is commonly referred to by its correct name of Nassfield Lock.

Notice the standard brick chamber with the local limestone capping. The white stones in the lockside are from nearby Rodborough, the red ones from Gatcombe in the Forest of Dean and the grey stones from Hanham near Bath.

Above the lock there is an interesting three arched culvert flowing underneath the towing path which conveys surplus water from the long Stonehouse pound to the pound below Nassfield Lock. The sill level here is at the same height as that which held up the old gates. Like the lock, the weir is built of local brick and limestone.

A few yards above Nassfield Lock the canal bears a little to the right, and the road bears a little to the left through the tiny hamlet of Newtown. Detailed research in this area over the last few years suggests some interesting possibilities about the origin of this settlement. Notice, first of all, the unusual absence of a church or any obvious village centre. Secondly, a brief look at the orientation of the houses confirms that originally they all faced the canal and not the road. Thirdly, all the houses are of a comparable age and this is confirmed by an examination of house deeds. This suggests the village has all grown up at the same time rather than evolved gradually over a longer period of time. Fourthly, all the houses are of comparable styles, built of comparable bricks and sometimes have the same detailed features. Nevertheless, there is a clearly marked division between the houses near the canal and the smaller cottages on the other side of the road. Fifthly, the three larger houses bear more than a passing resemblance to the lock house at Framilode, Dock House, Chippenham Platt Wharf and Ryeford Double Lock. Sixthly, all the smaller houses have long and large gardens stretching down towards the stream. It is clear from the 1:10000 scale map that the area incorporating these cottages and gardens was originally a single field. Seventhly, this hamlet of less than ten houses supported three public houses in the late eighteenth and early nineteenth centuries. These included Beech Cottage on the canal bank, the old New Inn next door painted in an unfortunate shade of flaking cream, and Mrs. Paskey's small end terrace house nearest Chippenham Platt. Finally the name of the hamlet itself suggests that what we are looking at is the 'new town' created by a navvies

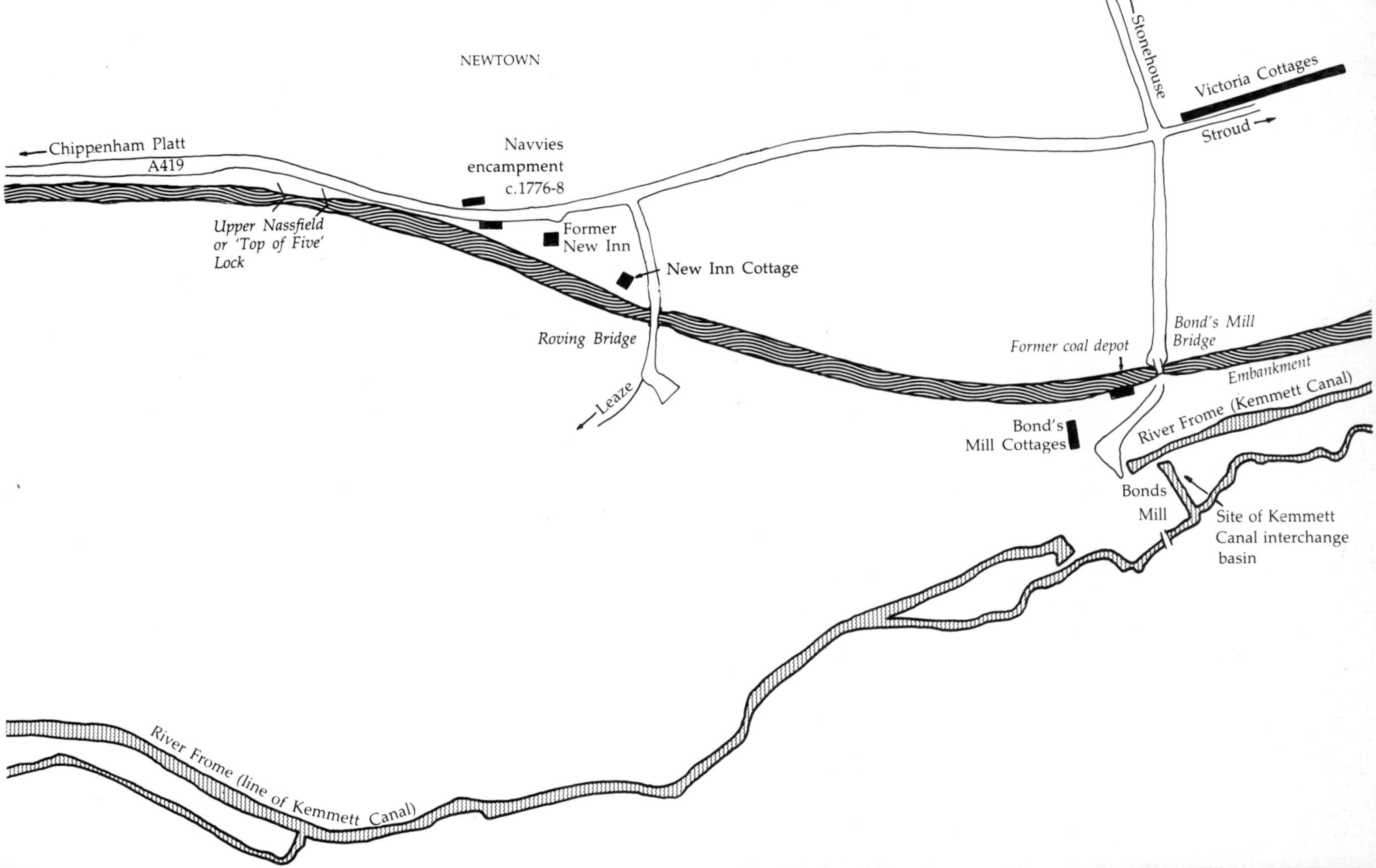

NEWTOWN

Chippenham Platt
A419

Navvies encampment
c.1776-8

Former
New Inn

New Inn Cottage

Upper Nassfield
or 'Top of Five'
Lock

Roving Bridge

Leaze

Victoria Cottages

Stroud

Stonehouse

Bond's Mill
Bridge

Embankment

River Frome (Kemmett Canal)

Former coal depot

Bond's
Mill Cottages

Bonds
Mill

Site of Kemmett
Canal interchange
basin

River Frome (line of Kemmett Canal)

encampment built around 1777–8.

The three larger houses on the canal bank could have been built by the Canal Company or its major shareholders as accommodation for its senior staff and craftsmen. The smaller cottages may have been intended for its junior craftsmen. The long gardens could be the site of makeshift temporary accommodation for its navvies employed on the major constructional jobs of the five locks and the long Stonehouse pound. If a fledgling canal company were thinking of providing a navvies camp it would in any case be logical to place it somewhere about halfway along the canal, especially if there were several large scale jobs nearby. It is perhaps not without significance that at least one Stroudwater director became involved with Stroud Brewery. The hostelries built at Newtown may have been the initial connection. Navvies restoring the canal today will recall too, that the Trust itself considered buying property here and basing its own maintenance depot at Newtown.

At the Roving Bridge, originally called Nassfield Bridge, the towpath crosses the canal and returns to the downside bank once more. Walk to the top of the bridge and take a good look round from this vantage point.

9. Eastington Bridge c. 1928. Early boating on 'Melody', a pleasure cruiser.
This replacement bridge was completed in 1924. The coal on the bank came
from Coppice Colliery in Staffordshire.

CHAPTER FIVE

The Kemmett Canal

On your walk from the River Severn to Meadow Bridge it has often been possible to follow the routes of the Kemmett and Stroudwater Canals at the same time. Sometimes, as at Framilode and Saul, they have been close together. Sometimes, as between Bristol Road and Westfield, there are no remains of one canal and so you have followed the line of the other instead. However, from Meadow Bridge where you are standing now, to Bonds Mill at Stonehouse the two canals are a couple of hundred yards apart. Consequently if you want to follow the route of John Kemmett's unique container canal you will need to use these directions and then retrace your steps.

As you approached Meadow Bridge the Kemmett Canal was on your immediate left. It runs under Meadow Bridge and upstream towards Churchend Mill in a straight line. It is difficult to believe now that this small branch of the River Frome is the only known case of a waterway originally constructed entirely with cranes instead of locks to effect the change in level, and the earliest known use of container traffic on any canal.

Walk through the stile on the left hand side of Meadow Bridge as you face upstream and follow the line of the footpath towards Churchend Mill. The Kemmett Canal is on your right. You can see in neighbouring fields on the far side of the canal the old lines of this branch of the Frome. This straightening is probably John Kemmett's work around 1759-60. Unfortunately, detailed proof of construction only goes as far upstream as Meadow Bridge itself, although other documentary inferences and evidence on the ground suggest it reached Stonehouse before being abandoned in 1763.

Pass through the stile at Churchend and turn right into the lane for a hundred yards or so. Just before the bridge over the Kemmett Canal you will see a pair of double metal gates on your left. If these are open walk in and ask the Tudor family if you may follow the canal line. *This is private land so do not proceed without permission and make sure all dogs are kept on a lead*. If the gates are closed or there is no-one about walk back to Churchend village a hundred yards or so away and call at Ian Tudor's house called Quercus. He will usually be able to provide you with a key to the gates in exchange for £1 returnable deposit.

Walk through the double metal gates keeping to the straight path ahead of you. The Kemmett Canal is on your right. Notice the stone edgings which continue for some distance. These probably date from the nineteenth century improvements to the water courses here. Follow the path through the gardens as far as the weir a hundred yards or so ahead. Stand on the stone and concrete bridge here looking downstream from the weir. John Kemmett's unorthodox container boats came up the stream here. The interchange basin with its crane was on your left. It is not certain if the present depression visible there was the actual basin. If not, it is certainly on the precise site where boats would moor ready for their container boxes to be lifted out of the hold, swung across the bank to your left and into one of the two small man-hauled boats which operated on each separate pound.

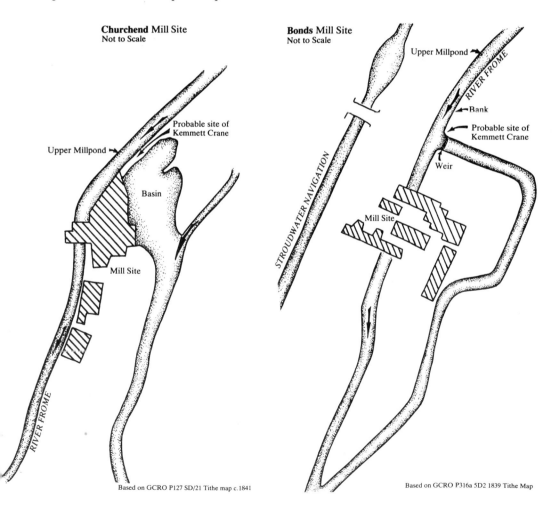

Churchend Mill Site
Not to Scale

Upper Millpond →

Probable site of
Kemmett Crane

Basin

Mill Site

RIVER FROME

Based on GCRO P127 SD/21 Tithe map c.1841

Bonds Mill Site
Not to Scale

Upper Millpond →

RIVER FROME

← Bank

Probable site of
Kemmett Crane

Weir

STROUDWATER NAVIGATION

Mill Site

Based on GCRO P316a 5D2 1839 Tithe Map

73

Continue along the pathway. The bank you are walking on was rebuilt in the nineteenth century, so there are no remains left of the iron cranes. The lower level of the Kemmett Canal is on your right and ends here as at each interchange. The upper level, taking the canal on to the next mill, is on your left. Keeping to the path you can follow the Kemmett Canal for several hundred yards as far as the point where a small weir stream bounded by a hedge leaves the canal. The later Stroudwater Canal is on the other side of the hill on your left.

Retrace your steps to the double metal gates and return the key to Ian Tudor. If these gates are locked and Ian Tudor is not available cross over the Kemmett Canal instead, and turn immediate left through the stile. Churchend Mill, now demolished, was on your left. You can hear the weir as you approach and see the layout of river, mill and canal on the plan of Churchend Mill site on page 73.

John Kemmett's Canal circumvented each mill site to avoid upsetting millowners, used cranes instead of locks so no water would be used and transferred cargo to the higher mill stream pound above each mill. So, as you walk up the footpath the canal has left the small watercourse on your left and is now on the upper stream marked by the line of willows about fifty yards beyond.

Follow the footpath round the corner. The small watercourse flows out of the upper stream here. The Kemmett Canal is now clearly visible again on your immediate left. The footpath now runs roughly parallel to the canal as far as Bonds Mill which is visible about two hundred yards further on. As you approach the mill the Frome divides. As usual, the Kemmett Canal goes round the mill using the overflow stream. It followed the watercourse nearest to you.

Further on the canal turns sharp left under a wood and steel flat bridge. Stop here and look up to the weir. The canal followed the standard pattern here – a crane and interchange basin to the right of the weir where cargoes were lifted into other boats running separately on the higher level. The plan on page 73 shows the layout here with the Kemmett Canal on the right of the page. The present Stroudwater Canal is on the hillside behind the mill. You can just see it marked by a line of willows near the top of the hill.

Retrace your steps to Meadow Bridge, turn right onto the road and back to Roving bridge. You can see the route of John Kemmett's Canal from Bonds Mill to Stonehouse from a better vantage point.

CHAPTER SIX

Roving Bridge to Ryeford Double Lock

Roving Bridge is a typical Stroudwater canal bridge. It has stone foundations which protrude slightly at water level to protect the bridge while the trows or long boats went through. Apart from the nineteenth-century coping bricks made from Staffordshire clay by Woods of Oldbury and brought here by water, the bridge is built entirely of original bricks. When the trows came upstream the boat men let the rope go from the craft. The man leading the mule coiled this up and took the animal across the bridge and down the small path which leads right up to the bridge at water level on the Stroud side. Meanwhile the trow drifted slowly underneath the bridge. The man standing on this small path threw the rope back to the boat and hitched the other end on to the mule once more. Mules, or 'hanimals' as they were called, was the usual means of hauling trows along the Stroudwater Canal after the horse towing path was put in during the mid 1820s. Before then men hauled the trows by hand. Mules were invariably even-tempered creatures much preferred by the trowmen to the more excitable donkeys commonly used for the long boats.

Standing on the bridge you can get a good view of Newtown, the East Lodge entrance to Eastington Park and the canal curving away towards Bonds Mill. Walking along the towpath you will come to a short stretch with new fencing and an absence of vegetation. This marks the line of the Milk Marketing Board culvert from the large factory on Oldlands Lane, Stonehouse, underneath the canal to the River Frome.

Further on the canal appears to enter a shallow cutting. If you look across to the offside of the canal you can see the original level of the land with the canal running down the top of the spur. On the towpath side the original profile of the adjacent field has been changed by the long standing deposition of canal dredgings. There is a blue bricked indentation in the canal bank nearer Bonds Mill. Its function is unknown.

As you draw level with Bonds Mill look out for the double wrought iron gates on cast iron pillars in the fence on the towpath side. Bonds Mill was originally a woollen mill and this gateway was installed to allow the coal to be unloaded directly into the mill. When the boats moored up here to unload they swung a plank across the towpath. One end rested on the gunwales of the boat and the other on a cart

positioned between the two gates. Boatmen then used shovels to fill a
wheelbarrow with coal, ran it along the plank suspended a few feet
above the towing path and tipped the coal into the waiting cart. The
horse and cart then carried the coal into a bunker ready for use in the
nearby boiler house. The coal bunker at Bonds Mill is the brick building
adjacent to the towpath fence.

The corrugated iron sides are a modern addition. All the mills along
the canal had coal bunkers of one sort or another for storing the fuel.
Sometimes they were small covered buildings like this but more
commonly they were simple open stone built enclosures similar to those
at Meadow Mill or Ryeford.

Bonds Mill Bridge will need replacing with a new moveable swing
bridge as restoration proceeds. The coping around the bridge is Cotswold limestone probably from nearby Rodborough Hill. After over two
centuries of use it is still in sound condition. There is a bench mark just
east of the bridge. During recent dredging here, volunteers found a
culvert on the towpath side beneath the bridge drained into the Frome.

The brick two storey pill box was installed during the war when Bonds
Mill was engaged on secret defence work. It was designed for use as a
machine gun position in case of invasion.

For the next mile or so the canal is built along the edge of the spur

*10. Pike Lock, Eastington c. 1910. John White, lock-keeper, is on the right.
Notice the lock gate construction and planks to protect them from damage by
passing craft.*

with a steep drop towards the valley bottom. The land between the towpath and the river as far as the railway bridge was used from early days for tipping canal dredgings. This served the double function of disposing of unwanted silt about midway along the canal and strengthening the bank at a vulnerable point. Regular tipping today would still be in the mutual interests of Canal Company and land owners. This would enrich the land and protect farmers from the serious damage of a potential burst.

There are the remains of a Stroudwater barge along this section which was built wide enough to allow two vessels with a 16' beam and each carrying about sixty tons to pass each other without difficulty.

Hoffmans Weir, installed in the 1950s to allow the mill to draw water from the canal, will need to be removed when navigation is restored. It will, in any case, be superfluous when the canal is restored to its original level.

In common with other towpath lengths this section was regularly made up with coal ash from the mill boilers.

Looking down the bank towards the valley you can see John Kemmett's Canal running parallel to the canal at the bottom of the towpath bank. Originally part of the mill stream for Bonds Mill, this stretch was utilised for his highly unorthodox canal between 1759 and 1763. The Frome now uses this length as one of its channels.

As you approach the railway bridge you pass through a towpath gate. The Stroudwater Canal had only a man towing path from 1775 to 1825 when both the Gloucester and Berkeley Canal Company and Thames & Severn Canal Company persuaded the Company to install a horse towing path. This was wider than the man towing path and had gates adapted for mule and donkey use. Man towing paths were unusual on artificial navigations but it was a logical decision for the young company to make when there were no other canals in the area. The Stroudwater was planned as a branch canal from the navigable River Severn and since this had no horse towing path at the time it was understandable that the new Canal Company followed the same pattern.

The woodland between the canal, railway embankment and Kemmett Canal belongs to the Canal Company. This too was used for dredgings for many years.

The bridge under the main line Birmingham to Bristol railway line has been filled in and Armco tubes are installed to provide pedestrian access along the towing path and allow the canal water to pass from one side of the bridge to the other. This major obstacle to restoration will need replacing by a box or circular culvert.

On the other side of the railway bridge the canal widens into an attractive area known as Stonehouse Ocean. Although sections of this are silted up, the whole area belongs to the Canal Company. There was

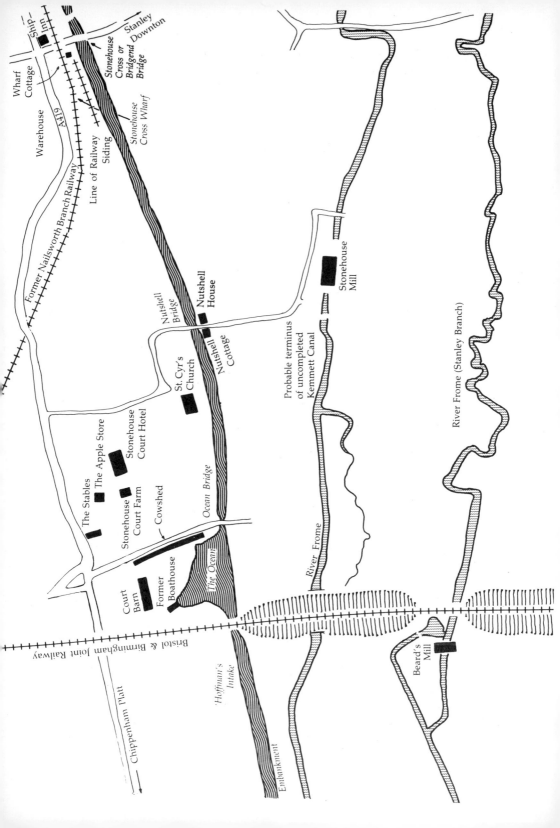

a boat repair yard in the far corner by the railway. It included a floating platform which raised boats out of the water for repair. A small feeder stream enters the canal nearby.

Originally the Ocean may have been no more than a winding hole. It was probably extended considerably to act as a wharf for railway building materials when the line was opened nearly a hundred and fifty years ago. It was certainly envisaged as an important canal and railway interchange wharf though there is little evidence it was used much for this function.

There were always two main types of craft on the canal and this pattern continued during the early years of this century. There were the boatmen running the Stroudwater barges and Severn trows bringing coal from Bullo Pill or Sharpness. This traffic came to canalside mills and gas works. These boatmen were invariably local men who could cycle home on the towpath in the evenings to Saul and other villages close to the canal, thus making the Ocean a popular overnight mooring place. The long distance coal traffic from Staffordshire to Chalford and other places along the Thames & Severn Canal came in long boats and were worked by families who lived on board. The swans, which have nested here for generations, make this an equally popular place for towpath walkers today.

Stonehouse Court Bridge, now commonly called Ocean Bridge, was another of the iron swingbridges installed in the 1880s to replace earlier wooden swing bridges. These bridges invariably swung from the offside to prevent the large iron level used to swing the bridge from obstructing the towpath side. Figure 34 in *The Stroudwater Canal* illustrates the original bridge structure and shows the lever clearly. At Ocean Bridge you can still see the recess into which the bridge swung. The bridge is set between two large sandstone copings probably from Gatcombe on the River Wye. The holes made for the ironwork are visible too. The Cotswold limestone copings either side of the sandstone and on the offside came from the same source as those at Bonds Mill. Stonehouse Court was originally a Tudor house but was burnt down and redesigned by Sir Edward Lutyens. It is now an excellent country hotel serving afternoon teas while its canal orientated Buttery Bar serves moderately priced hot and cold country food at lunchtime, and in the evenings walkers will find the Buttery Bar menu good value; food eaten in the Buttery Bar from the upstairs dining room menu is more expensive.

Go through the gate in the wall facing the canal near Ocean Bridge, up the path, through the back door on the ground floor and turn left inside. The attractive church of St. Cyr nearby lost part of its churchyard when the canal was constructed.

Turning round and looking down into the Frome valley you can see where John Kemmett's Canal, nearest the towpath, and the River Frome join forces once again. There is plenty of visual evidence here of river straightening possibly undertaken by Kemmett's navvies. This was the furthest point this unusual canal penetrated up the valley before it was abandoned. There is no evidence to suggest whether or not this length was ever used by the container boats before the work was suspended in 1763.

Nutshell Cottage, House and Bridge remain an enigma. The design suggests they were built together *c.* 1778 and used as a type of 'look out' residence by the Canal Company. Nevertheless there seems no reason *why* the Company should require such a facility at this point. There are no locks, Company run wharves, maintenance yards, toll houses, swing bridges or any other function which would benefit from such an expenditure by a hard pressed Canal Company. There is no documentary evidence in any of the deeds, minutes or elsewhere to suggest it was ever owned by them or had any connection with the Company.

There is a small early nineteenth-century walled-in garden around Nutshell Cottage. A stone lintel in the wall suggests a door once led

11. Roving Bridge, Newtown 1973. Here the towing path crosses from one side of the canal to the other.

from the towpath to the garden. On the Stroud side of the bridge there was a coal pen in the garden of Nutshell House used for storing coal for Stanley Mill. There is also a tunnel underneath the bridge abutment linking the two residences together. Locals suggest that Nutshell Cottage was constructed as navvies accommodation but this is debatable. It remains conceivable the Company built these two dwellings to accommodate carpenters and stonemasons using the larger garden of Nutshell House for temporary navvies dwellings. If any towpath walker has further thoughts on this puzzle I would be grateful to hear from them.

Nutshell Bridge is original and carries a private road to Stanley Mills. It has been repaired with Staffordshire blue bricks at various times.

The canal now runs in a straight line as far as Stonehouse Cross Wharf and Bridgend Bridge. The bridge itself has been demolished, and a new brick structure will be needed here to replace the Armco tubes. The long stretch of land on the offside, now occupied by a lorry firm, is the wharf. This acquired the name Penn's Wharf during the early twentieth century when it was leased by Mr. Penn. He sold steam coal brought from the Forest by trows, and domestic coal from Staffordshire brought by long boats. Unlike Smarts of Chalford, he owned no boats himself, but bought regularly chartered cargoes from boat owners. During the early nineteenth century the *Stroud Packet* used this wharf to deliver groceries it collected on its weekly run to Bristol. Later on the name was changed to the *Bounty.*

Several locals recall a distinction between the mostly Saul-based 'gentlemen trowmen' and the 'layabout boatmen' from the midlands-based long boats. These boatmen are remembered as inclined to drink to excess and be cruel to children and animals. It is not certain if this was a common distinction or, more likely, only occasionally true. Fred Rowbotham, the present Canal Company engineer, recalls that while long boat cabin interiors were always decorated they were not usually decorated externally until trade began to fall off.

The wharf house is boarded up and neglected. Looking back down the canal to Nutshell House you can see there are certain similarities with the house here. Both have the same yellow quoins and the same yellow string brick courses. This brick patterning is a common feature of this part of the Frome valley and does not necesssarily imply they were both constructed by the same builder.

Since the boats were all unloaded by hand into carts the coal wharf was near to the bridge and road to minimize distances the carts had to travel.

The Ship Inn on the offside bank on the Stroud side of the bridge has forgotten its earlier associations with the canal. Sadly it turns its back on the water.

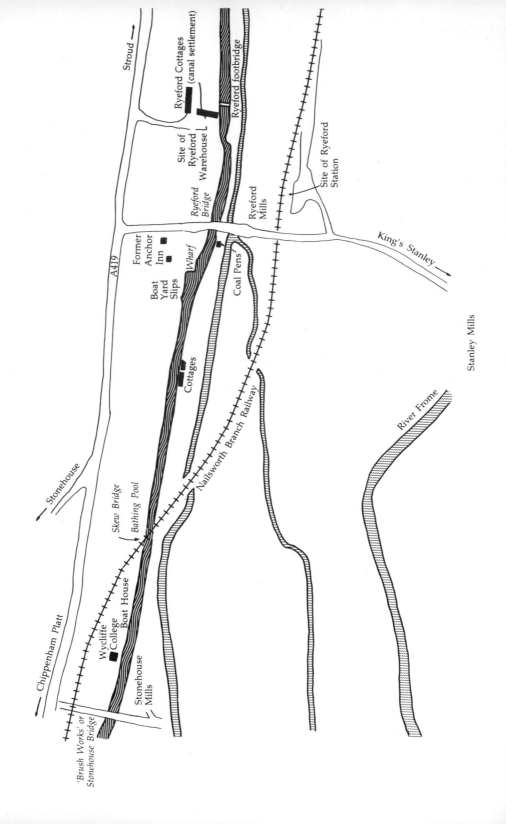

It is easy to get into Stonehouse from this point and regular bus and train services run on to Stroud or back to Gloucester.

The original swing bridge at Upper Mill has been replaced by a fixed structure though the stately entrance gates to the former woollen mills, now the Stonehouse Industrial Estate, remain. There is no evidence here of a coal pen, perhaps because the mill was so close fuel was unloaded directly into the boiler room. A few yards further on you can see the boathouse used by Wycliffe College when the canal was navigable.

Nearer the railway bridge carrying the old branch line from Stonehouse to Nailsworth, development by the new chemical works mars the canalside scene. Despite instructions to the contrary they have allowed their access road and car park to encroach on Canal Company land. The rubbish stewn areas round the factory is unfortunate This stretch towards the attractive iron railway bridge was once a popular spot for swimming. There are the remains of a swimming hut on the offside just before the bridge.

The two stone built rows of cottages on the canal bank a little further on were probably owned by one of the local mills. There is no known connection with the canal apart from the arch in the side of the building which was used to unload canal-borne coal directly into the cellar.

There are two more coal pens on the towpath near Ryeford Bridge.

12. Wycliffe College boathouse, Stonehouse c. 1925.

The first belonged to Stanley Mills and the other to Ryeford Mills. Notice how the gateway is just wide enough for a horse and cart. The usual 'plank and wheelbarrow' unloading techniques was used here with the plank running from the boat to the top of the coal pen wall or, if the pen were empty, directly into the waiting horse and cart.

On the offside the remains of the two double ended trows *Perseverance* and *Severn Bridge* were visible until recent years. The stone built house formerly the Anchor Inn, has been converted into a private dwelling called Tankard House. The brick buildings nearer the bridge belonged to the important Ryeford Wharf – one of the largest wharves on the canal. At various times the wharf buildings included a bakery, shop, and cabinet makers. The coal was stored between the canal and the wharf houses.

The two sides of Ryeford Bridge present different aspects. The Stroud side, with its keystone, is original. The red brick bridge has been extended on the other side using similar bricks. There is some evidence of towing marks on the bridge here though it was more usual for mules to go over the road and down on to the towpath on the other side. These original Stroudwater bridges were not designed to provide space for animals to tow the boats under them. When the horse towing path was installed the Company tried first to provide the extra height by dropping the towpath a few inches beneath the bridge but more often than not this led to the towpath being flooded.

Bearing in mind the Stroud barges were large wide-beamed craft requiring two or three donkeys to pull them, it requires little imagination to see how difficult it would be to manœuvre three of them under Ryeford Bridge at once without the risk of accidents. Since the Company wished to avoid the expense of rebuilding some of its brick bridges boatmen were obliged to use the less convenient method of unhitching the mules, taking them across the road and down to the canal again on the other side. Notice the mooring rings in the canal bank east of Ryeford Bridge.

Near the small footbridge opposite Ryeford Corn Mills there is a delightful canalside settlement. These cottages were probably built for boatmen and canal workers. There has been some encroachment on the canal by householders' gardens here.

The towpath from here to Ryeford Double Locks runs on a narrow ledge between the canal and the River Frome. Notice the equipment for the use of water power in Ryeford Saw Mills on your right. The land now rises steeply to your left as you approach the locks. There is a good photograph taken *c.*1906 reproduced in Plate 30 of *The Stroudwater Canal.*

CHAPTER SEVEN

Ryeford Double Lock to Wallbridge

The impressive Double Lock at Ryeford, started in March 1779, was completed three months later at a cost of £760. Designed by Anthony Keck, the local Kings Stanley architect, it followed the usual pattern of canal construction. Each major structure such as locks and bridges were separately designed as the work proceeded. Each part of the work – cutting, stone foundations, brickwork, gates and ironwork – was supplied by different subcontractors.

Shortly after the canal was opened in July 1779 the north wall of this lock collapsed. This was caused by water pressure from the higher offside land causing the wall to bulge. Keck lost the subsequent court case and was obliged to rebuild the lock at his own expense installing circular drainage trunks to drain the land and reduce the water pressure. These trunks are visible on the offside above and below the lock.

The company-built lockhouse is similar in style to other houses at Framilode, Bristol Road, Chippenham Platt and elsewhere. A small brick building at the rear has a fireplace and may have been used as temporary accommodation for masons, foreman bricklayers and the like during construction of the lock. Extensive recently unearthed evidence of food detritus suggests the entire gardens behind the lockhouse were used as a navvies encampment. From the Double Lock to Dudbridge Locks the canal was built two feet deeper than the rest of the canal, to act as a reservoir holding an extra seventy-four locks of water. The pound from Dudbridge to Wallbridge was also built three feet deeper with the same purpose in mind to hold an extra ninety locks of water.

From a short distance above the Double Locks the canal is infilled for almost a mile. Ebley Saw Mills is on the offside a little further on. The former wharf here has the base of an old Stroudwater crane standing up about twelve feet next to the canal. An old wooden pile driver nearby has now been destroyed. The warehouse standing at right-angles to the canal may originally have been built by the Canal Company. Within living memory it was used for stables and as living accommodation. The two small brick buildings on the offside a little further on were stables and a hayloft.

On the towpath side here you can see another of the unusual circular weirs probably installed by Thomas Dadford junior. There is a second

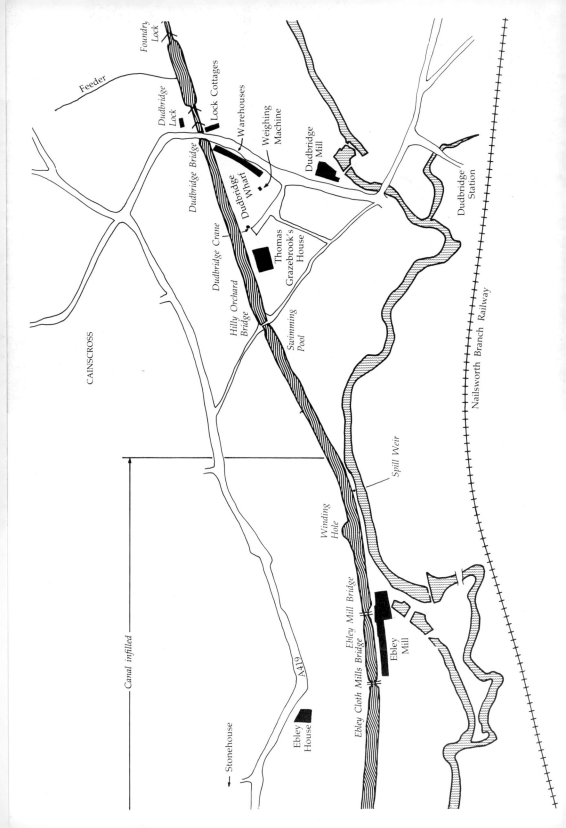

Ebley Mills. Stroud

need to include provision for a new swing bridge to maintain vehicular access between both banks of the waterway.

Leaving the Ebley Mills site there was a large winding hole on the offside. This was situated near the line of willows going up the fence by the first house past the mills. Notice the remains of the canal overflow weir into the river nearby. Follow the line of the towpath and cross over the concrete bridge at the end of the infilled section. Looking back down the canal notice how the tree in the dip marks the offside line of the canal.

From here to the Hilly Orchard footbridge the canal runs in a straight line. There is an excellent photograph of the trow Gertrude taken at this bridge c. 1900 on page 206 of Charles Hadfield's *The Canals of South and South Eastern England*. The towpath from here to Dudbridge Locks is passable with difficulty. An alternative route is to turn right at Hilly Orchard, past the small houses facing you, then left and out on to the main road walking as far as Dudbridge Locks and back onto the canal. If you take this route notice the old canal weighbridge house on the main road at the entrance to Dudbridge Wharf.

If you decide to follow the towing path route you will find the canal hidden behind high walls which makes visibility difficult. A hundred

14. Ebley Mills c. 1910. Notice the 'kissing gates' on the towpath to prevent animals straying.

yards or so further on you will reach a large listed stonebuilt property standing at right angles to the canal. This is Gladfield Gardens. The house was built by Thomas Grazebrook in the late eighteenth century and eventually passed to the coal carrying Ward family when they ran the adjacent wharf. This house and many other small dwellings nearby were probably part of a small settlement based on work available at the wharf here. Wards sold the wharf around 1930 and the last load of coal was delivered here about 1940.

A little further on you can see the only remaining Stroudwater crane still in position. It is marked 'John Stevenson, Canal Foundry, Preston', and is believed to have been installed about 1820. Its current owner, Mr. Wiggall, might be prepared to see the crane removed to a renovated Wallbridge Conservation Area. The wharf area is now separated from

15. Ebley Mills and the infilled canal 1973.

90

the canal by a high wall but the old Dudbridge warehouse and the weighbridge building still stand on the wharf and main road respectively.

At Dudbridge you can get along the towpath with difficulty. The west side of this original bridge has been extended and faced with stone. Underneath the bridge there are the iron remains of a rubbing strip to prevent ropes catching on the stonework. There is also an iron hook beneath the bridge probably used to tie up the boats while the lock was made ready.

The towpath rises steeply to Dudbridge Locks. Notice the 1778 date on the keystone on the Stroud side and the original water level clearly marked by the colour of the brickwork.

The two locks at Dudbridge, called originally Franklin's Locks, then Upper and Lower Dudbridge and finally Dudbridge and Foundry Lock were built by William Franklin between April 1778 and the spring of 1779. The Company probably decided to build these locks before the Ryeford Double Lock to help persuade shareholders to raise an additional sum of money when the original estimates were exceeded. Working at Dudbridge would suggest the canal was approaching completion and that further shareholder investment was worthwhile.

The two cottages behind you on the towpath were lock cottages, one of which was last occupied by 'Bargey' Bassett. They are both in poor condition and may be demolished shortly. The houses on the offside have no known connections with the canal, although there is a suspicion one of them was a beer house frequented by boatmen. The function of the stone wall, built near the top gate and using the same stone as the bridge, remains a mystery.

Dudbridge lock is brick built with stone coping. Notice once again the iron rubbing straight on the lockside to minimise wear. At Foundry Lock notice how the brickwork on the lower offside has been shaped to take the gate paddle. The ironwork embedded in the stone lock coping was used for securing the gates. The small stream from the millpond of the former corn mill now runs into the canal, but originally ran underneath to the Frome. On the 1902 Ordnance Survey map two small buildings are marked on the towpath side here. These may have been lock houses.

A new access bridge has been built across the canal in the next pound to give access to the playing fields. Walking up the towpath you approach the site of the former Stroud Gas Works. The last boat to use the canal unloaded ten tons of coal at the Gas Works Wharf in 1941. You can see the position of the wharf from the length of blue bricks on the towpath side at the edge of the road. Originally the wharf was probably edged with stone.

Gas Works Swing Bridge, a few yards further on, retains the original brickwork and stone work. The small stone built house on the offside

was two cottages at an earlier date. This was the Dudbridge Coal Wharf and the coal was piled on the area now occupied by the lawn. There is some similarity between the stone work of this house and the former Company headquarters at Wallbridge. It may, therefore, have been built at the same time with some surplus stone left over from the Wallbridge building. There has been a small amount of land encroachment here and this will need clearing when the canal is restored through this pound. The larger brick house on the other side of the lane was built by the gas company as a home for their manager.

The canal now bends slightly to the right. On the offside are the remains of the large millpond for Lodgemore Mills. It drains underneath the canal into the River Frome. The canal took part of this millpond during construction so the pond was rebuilt 'lengthened and thinned' to provide the same water storage. The swingbridge here has been fixed and like several others will need rebuilding to permit through navigation.

Just below the junction of the Painswick Stream on the offside the brick wall curves inland. This is the site of a former winding hole and boathouse for the company pleasure boat used by directors for their annual inspection. The Painswick Stream enters the canal here and provides a substantial source of water supply for the canal. Originally it

16. Ebley Cloth Mills Swing Bridge c. 1906. The boathouse suggests local pleasure use of the canal.

drained underneath the navigation, and into a millpond just south of the canal. There is some evidence to suggest that small, flat-bottomed raft-like craft operated on the Painswick Stream carrying grains and oils to and from Stratford Mill about 500 yards north of the canal on the banks of the stream. These materials were unloaded over the offside canal bank and onto the rafts perhaps using some primitive type of crane. A single flash lock, marked sluice on the 1902 Ordnance Survey Map, was positioned about halfway up this simple navigation. In all probability it comprised nothing more substantial than planks placed across the stream to build up a head of water.

During seasonal water shortages, or other periods of low water, the boatmen operating on the Painswick Stream used a well-established method of providing additional depth. This involved dragging sailcloth a few inches downstream of the boat to help back up the water level in the same way as the boatmen used it in the upper reaches of the River Wye. In essence this was a sort of moveable instant flash lock which

17. Victoria Inn (now demolished) stood alongside Foundry Lock at Dudbridge about 200 yards below Stroud Gas Works. Annie Clark was the licensee. The site is now part of Marling School playing fields. Taken c. 1954.

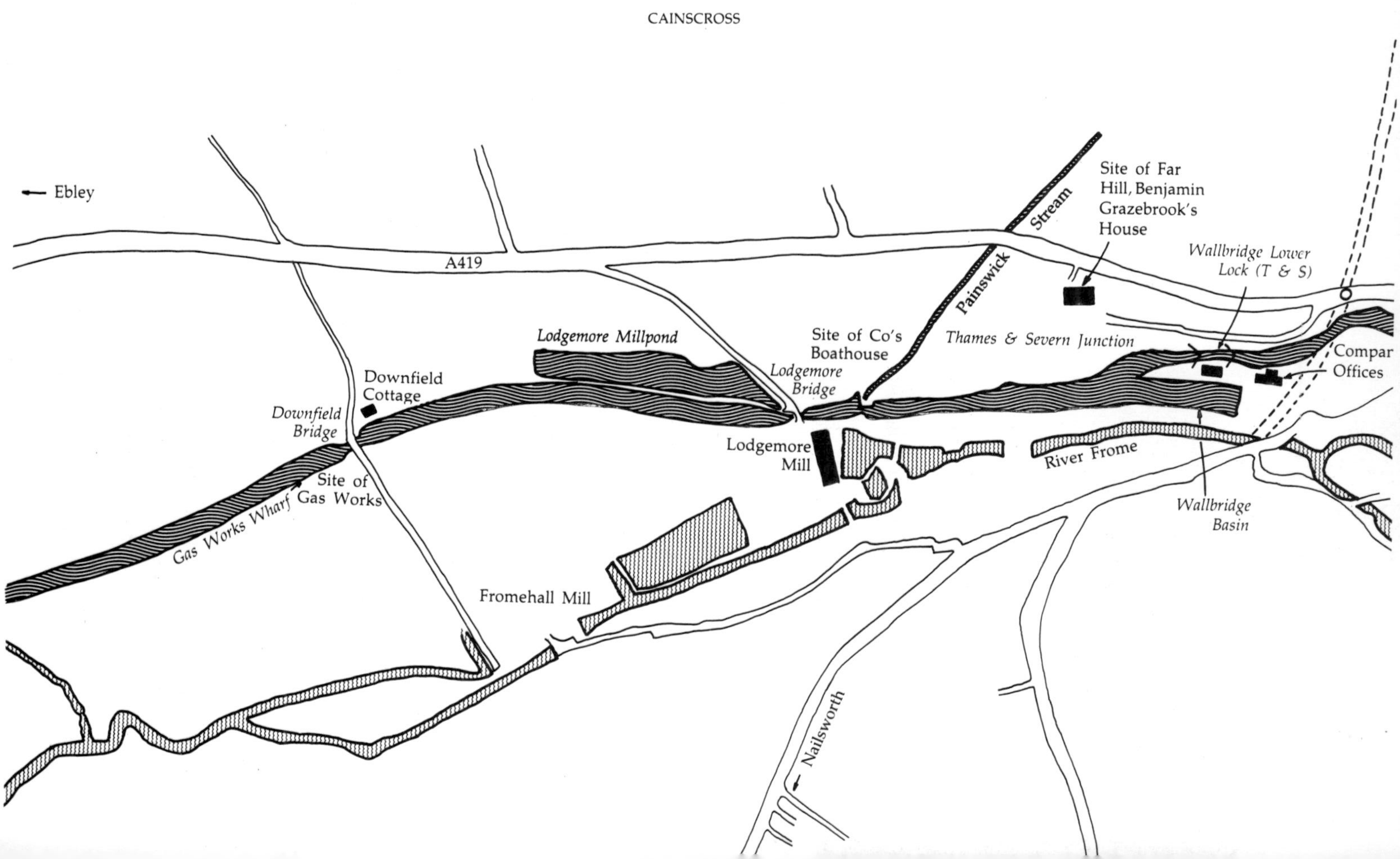

CAINSCROSS

Ebley

A419

Palmswick Stream

Thames & Severn Junction

Site of Far Hill, Benjamin Grazebrook's House

Wallbridge Lower Lock (T & S)

Compar Offices

Wallbridge Basin

River Frome

Site of Co's Boathouse

Lodgemore Bridge

Lodgemore Mill

Lodgemore Millpond

Nailsworth

Fromehall Mill

Downfield Cottage

Downfield Bridge

Site of Gas Works Wharf Gas Works

Gas Works

gave extra depth when and where it was required. Presumably man towage was common on the Painswick Stream but mules may have been used on occasions.

As you continue along the towpath you pass the brick built Lodgemore Mills Works on the right. Walk through the door set in the towpath. On the offside at this point there was a winding hole but this is no longer visible.

You are now approaching the terminus of the canal at Wallbridge. Far Hill, Benjamin Grazebook's great house stood on the opposite bank until it was demolished a few years ago. Grazebrook started life as a local small scale contractor and engineer. He bought a few shares in the Canal Company in 1774, became under-surveyor, Company Clerk and successively influential committee member, engineer, proprietor of Grazebook and Co. – the principal carriers on the canal – joint owner of Stroud Bank and Stroud Brewery and chairman of the Canal Company. Benjamin Grazebrook is undoubtedly the single most influential and significant entrepreneur in the history of the town. It is unfortunate that Far Hill, his once magnificent house with its lantern lit grounds running down to his canal, should fall into the hands of Stroud District Council in 1973 and be demolished. A scheme for preserving it and turning the former grounds into a park was an alternative option.

From this point onwards the towpath was well supplied with posts for mooring barges and trows. The land between the canal and river formed

18. Lodgemore Swing Bridge c. 1907. Another iron swing bridge replacing earlier wooden ones. Notice the trow and Company warehouse in the distance.

part of a large wharf. The Thames & Severn Canal leaves the Stroud-water Canal at this point and runs behind the former coal wharf, the Company warehouse and former Canal Company headquarters. Wallbridge Basin was infilled in 1954 and is now owned by the Severn Trent Water Authority, but it is easy to trace the former outline. There are the remains of a cast iron crane base, probably identical to the one at Dudbridge, close to the wire fence at the Stroud end of the basin.

The warehouse, now owned by J.F. Hopson Ltd., was built by the Canal Company around 1780. Notice the stone lintels. Inappropriate tiles have replaced a Welsh slate roof. Until it was demolished a few years ago, there was a small weighbridge house between the warehouse and Canal Company headquarters. The weighing machine stood on the south side of the house.

The imposing stone built building facing the basin was built by William Franklin in 1795-7 for the Canal Company and was used as their headquarters until it was sold in 1953-4. The offices were in the left-hand-room looking on to the Thames & Severn Canal. The room in the centre of the ground floor was used for committee meetings. It would today still make a superb headquarters for a rejuvenated Canal Company, an active canal trust and perhaps the yet unformed Cotswold Canals Trust.

The buildings on the other side of the new road at Wallbridge probably all date from soon after the canal was rebuilt. They include a former cloth mill (No. 12) a blacksmith who shod barge horses (No. 11) and an old bakery (No. 8). The Old Ship Inn, lying alongside the Frome at the corner of the basin nearest the road, has left no trace. RJD Fine Arts at 12 Wallbridge is well worth a visit. They are building up a collection of canal pictures and prints. Wallbridge, the old port of Stroud, is today a run-down area with a number of important architectural buildings and enormous potential. It would make a superb conservation area. Sadly Wallbridge stands in silent reproach to thoughtless and unnecessary neglect.

CHAPTER EIGHT

The Thames & Severn Canal – Historical Outline

Gloucester November 19th 1789

This day was effected the greatest object of internal navigation in this kingdom. The Severn was united to the Thames, by an intermediate canal ascending by Stroud through the vale of Chalford to a height of 343 feet by 28 locks; there entering a tunnel through the hill of Sapperton for the length of two miles and three furlongs, and descending 134 feet by 14 locks it joined the Thames near Lechlade.

. . . this undertaking is worthy of a great commercial nation, and does great credit to the exertions of the individuals who have promoted and completed a work of such magnitude, at an expense of near two hundred thousand pounds.

Thus at least two of the national newspapers, including *The Times*, the local *Gloucester Journal*, and the influential *Gentleman's Magazine* recorded the opening of the Thames & Severn Canal. The full report, of which this is only an extract, captures effectively much of the contemporary wonder at the achievement, and we can gain considerable insight into the impact of this new canal by studying the words of contemporaries.

The idea to link the two great rivers of southern Britain was certainly not a new concept. For nearly two centuries before its actual achievement, local and national figures had been making suggestions and recommendations to create a link; their motivations varied, but all saw the potential benefits to trade in providing as direct an access as possible to the capital city on the Thames.

This is not the opportunity to study such proposals in detail, and indeed for this and all other aspects of the history of the Thames & Severn Canal one is recommended without hesitation to the study published under this title by Humphrey Household (new edition Alan Sutton 1983). Actually, an even greater body of information is contained within the same author's thesis for the University of Bristol on the T & S, subtitled 'birth and death of a canal'. All students are indeed doubly fortunate when approaching this canal because they not only have the fruits of twenty years research but also the great archive of original records (plans, notes, reports etc.) amassed by the Canal Company and preserved in the Gloucestershire Record Office. For detailed reference to particular aspects, one can do no better than return to these original sources.

Here we can only summarise some aspects of the written evidence as an introduction to the study (and enjoyment) of the Thames & Severn as it survives now on the ground. It will be obvious that the line is derelict and that the heyday of the canal was well over a century ago. In the period since abandonment of most of the line in 1927 and the remainder at the western end in 1933, so much has happened to relegate the canal as a forgotten aspect of commercial and transport history in the Cotswolds. Its former importance and significance might suggest that it deserves a better fate than oblivion, and indeed the current restoration activities of the Stroudwater, Thames & Severn Canal Trust are intended to restore something of the tarnished image, albeit for a very different type of use and user.

Before the eighteenth century, when the line actually adopted through the Frome valley and Stroud came to be chosen, proposals were advanced from time to time for other lines of connection between Severn and Thames. Their study on the ground would also be a fascinating exercise, not least because several would have crossed areas of un-doubted natural beauty not easily associated to the modern eye with canal construction. Indeed the adopted route was only just successful over an alternative line from Tewkesbury and Cheltenham, linking with the river Coln through Bibury and Fairford and thence to the Thames at Lechlade. Other routes also had their supporters and this searching for a successful line gives an indication of the enormity of the task of cutting through the Cotswold scarp at a suitable point.

The construction of Sapperton tunnel was regarded at the time, and has been ever since, as one of the engineering achievements of the day. It took five and a half years to build and extends over two and a quarter miles through the Cotswold hills. Its construction was riven with difficulties but the final achievement is symbolic not only of the energy and enthusiasm of eighteenth-century canal 'developers' but also of the construction gangs who risked life and limb (and occasionally lost both) to cut the line through. In fact, the actual period of construction of the T & S (virtually thirty miles in total length) was a mere six years and seven months, from the passing of the Act of authorisation on 17 April 1783. This compares well with progress on the ground made by other contemporary schemes and we must realise, of course, that many such schemes were themselves deadly rivals for the shortest and the quickest route between two centres. Hence the completion of the Thames & Severn late in 1789 came only a few months before the long-awaited completion of the Oxford Canal into Oxford in January 1790 and the junction between the Coventry and the Birmingham Canals in July that same year. All three were effectively competing for the route to London for west midland products and goods, and each was spurred on by the progress of its rival. In this aspect of the history of canals, the men who cut the Thames & Severn – and the promoters who financed the project – made a good account of themselves.

A meeting held in Cirencester in September 1781 to promote the idea of the canal proved to be the turning point; those involved decided very quickly to seek professional advice and they turned to a man who was probably the most outstanding canal engineer of the day, Robert Whitworth. He had been a pupil of Brindley, the great canal builder, and had developed his skills in draughtsmanship and site survey for various promotors of intended lines of canals, together with experience in canal engineering.

In fact when Whitworth was called in the Thames & Severn promoters were still divided on the best line for the canal and this and other reasons may have lain behind the rather nebulous instructions given to him in carrying out his survey. He was, for example, given no guidelines on the scale of the cut, and this was a particularly difficult problem in view of the three different sizes of vessels which were to be expected to use the through route when completed: the 12' width of the Thames barges, the 15' width of the Severn trows, and the narrower 7' variety of canal boat which later became ubiquitous on the canal system. In fact, Whitworth assumed that the dimensions required related to the Thames barge and that transhipment at one point would be necessary.

Whitworth visited Cirencester in December 1781 to conduct his survey, which was not however forthcoming for a further year as the result of commitments elsewhere. He made a further assumption of some significance: that an exact and thorough survey was not required of him. As a result he set out 'to form a proper judgement of the surveys already made' and to compare the practicability and expense of the alternative routes then under discussion. He found that the 'Cirencester line' – i.e. the line eventually selected and built – had a number of advantages; it would require a lower summit (hence less lockage) and it would have a total length of seven and a half miles less than the Tewkesbury-Cheltenham-Lechlade line. It was also noted that the water yield from the Churn and the Frome would far exceed that of the springs in the upper Coln Valley, leaving aside the additional difficulties of the latter route in access to water and problems with supplies to mills on the river. His estimate for the Cirencester line was £127,916. 4s. 0d. for a total of twenty-nine miles and three and a half furlongs.

The major problem noted in the report was a section where the line of the summit level ran 'over some bad rocky ground, which cannot be avoided for several miles altogether, that is worse than I have ever seen any canal cut through for such a continued length'. This proved to be a well-justified warning as subsequent efforts to retain an adequate supply of water in the summit level were to prove. Despite such difficulties and the distinct lack of measurement in detail for cutting the line (reservoirs, wharves, warehouses and water compensation costs were all excluded from the estimate), the promoters adopted this route in January 1783. Three months later came the passing of the Act and within weeks James Perry, the Company's first superintendant, had nearly 200 men at work along the line; on 10 June Charles Kinner, described as a 'navvy', was paid four shillings for 'Taking up a hedge'. From then on, the story is largely an account of the steady progress in construction working east from Stroud, together with the associated task of winning over the landowners along the line to ensure that work could proceed. The construction of the tunnel at Sapperton proved to be an even more hazardous and difficult enterprise than the promoters had imagined.

Amongst the most significant figures in this early construction period were Josiah Clowes, appointed to be the Company's 'surveyor and engineer and head carpenter' at a salary of £300 p.a., Samuel Smith, clerk of works and his assistant Richard Hall whose journal of memoranda from 1784-94 records something of the day-to-day problems and frustrations in building the canal. The detail of this period of activity is indeed fascinating and remains well preserved in the manuscript archives in Gloucester. We can only pick briefly from this record and the work of subsequent historians (see Further Reading). It seems clear that the proprietors of the Canal Company had hoped that Robert Whitworth would play a large role in the period of construction. In fact, apart from the initial survey (for which his fee was eighteen guineas) he did little other than mark out the line of the nine-mile long summit level which included, of course, Sapperton tunnel. This task alone took up fifty-six days for which he was paid £93. 7s. 6d.

It fell to Clowes to relate the feasibility scheme to the actual cut of the canal, and alterations and amendments which he made subsequently became a matter of controversy with the canal proprietors when mistakes appeared; the main example of this is the error in levels on either side of the summit, which can be seen to particular advantage in the close proximity of the locks climbing up to Daneway and the inadequate pounds between them. In addition Clowes bore the brunt of the many difficulties resulting from the selection of the hopelessly inadequate contractor Charles Jones to construct the Sapperton tunnel, and these problems contributed to the length of time it finally took to complete the tunnel.

The actual work of construction proceeded by a system described by Household as 'gang-piecework' under which gang leaders entered into agreements for each task undertaken. From this naturally developed the idea of contractors, men of sufficient experience, bearing or influence to undertake an agreed section of work for a fixed sum. It would be fascinating to know more about such men, nearly all of whom were self-made. On the Thames & Severn, it is possible to see from the records who was employed where and at what cost, and thus to build up a picture of the progress of the works and some of the individuals involved. A number, such as Thomas Cook and John Nock, both stonemasons, became contractors of some stature employing numbers of men. Equally, both were typical of such men travelling from one site contract to another, and indeed undertaking various contracts simultaneously. Cook had gained experience on the Stroudwater construction, and Nock on the Stourbridge Navigation; Cook's work on the Thames & Severn covered the period 1784-95 and included the building of the Brimscombe Port house, and (I suspect) the Coates portal of the Sapperton tunnel. During this same period he was the main contractor for the rebuilding of Gloucester Jail between 1786-91.

Many of the labourers' references are to 'day-works' – a still familiar term – and often indicate the nature of the work undertaken; thus Simon Hamer received £39. 17s. 7½d. on 14 July 1784 for 'day work and walling at Mr. Griffin' – i.e. Griffins Lock. A year later he was working regularly up at Daneway as the cutting approached the summit level. Other outside contractors are also mentioned, to complete the picture; John Wood, 'carrier at or near Cirencester' received £6. 16s. 0d. on 7 August 1786 for carrying 13,600 bricks from Siddington (brick yard) to the new feeder being constructed at Cirencester. A year's worth of mole-catching along the canal line earned Richard Musto the sum of four guineas in March 1795.

Thus the canal was built and subsequently maintained. There were numerous errors and examples of poor workmanship; some bridges fell down and had to be rebuilt, and later corrections were necessary to faults not appreciated at the time of construction. Thus Boxwell spring lock was constructed in 1792 to gain access to the water supplies from the nearby springs. Throughout its working life, the tasks of repair and maintenance formed a considerable problem for the proprietors of the Thames & Severn.

This is not the place to recount the history of trade on the Thames & Severn for the century of commercial activity from the arrival of the first boat into the Thames via Inglesham lock on 20 November 1789. Household's history summarises this admirably, and includes a summary of the dividends paid to shareholders from 1810 through to 1864 – a fairly consistent pattern until a distinct reduction in payments after the mid-1850s and no dividends paid at all after 1864. The pattern is, in fact, a more or less consistent downward trend thereafter; the continuing problems of maintenance, tackled with such determination at intervals during the first half of the nineteenth century, continued to drain resources thereafter.

By the time the canal's centenary came round, the prospects were distinctly unfavourable, and at the end of 1893 a notice was issued closing the canal east of Chalford until further notice. Regarded by many locally as an indication of imminent permanent closure, this episode stimulated the formation of a Trust consisting of six other canal companies and five local authorities. £18,000 was borrowed to finance major repair works and the entire canal length was re-opened in March 1899. Regrettably, this proved to be short-lived and the canal was closed at the summit three months later because of leakage.

These last few years of activity have left their mark on the canal for the towpath walker to detect today, particularly the next episode during the first decade of this century. Emerging from the debacle of the Trust as the most involved party, Gloucestershire County Council took over the canals in 1900 and set about a further programme of repairs involving in places a concrete re-lining of the canal bed. The section from Cirencester to the Thames was re-opened in the following year, the Stroud to Daneway length the next year and the summit level in January 1904. However, lengthy periods of closure for repairs in each of the next three years proved too great a strain, and a further closure of twelve weeks for the complete rebuilding at Pucks Mill Lower lock and the pound above in 1907 probably proved decisive in the minds of long suffering councillors.

So, the end was in sight; the record shows the last loaded boat (with stone) passing over the summit in May 1911, and thereafter only spasmodic repair work is recorded up to the outbreak of war. By 1927 when closure notices were issued from Whitehall Bridge for the summit and eastern sections, and again in 1933 for the remainder of the canal, there can have been little real objection to the inevitable demise of the through link from Severn to Thames. Another forty years were to pass before serious restoration proposals were canvassed again in Gloucestershire.

CHAPTER NINE

Wallbridge to Brimscombe Port

Wallbridge Junction to Bowbridge Lock.

The Thames & Severn Canal began in Stroud at the terminal basin of the Stroudwater Navigation at Wallbridge and by means of a side arm leading off the northern edge of the basin it fairly quickly ascended the Wallbridge Lower and Wallbridge Upper Locks to come to an area where the Company located its own Wallbridge Wharf. The junction site and the Lower Lock site are adjacent to the former Stroudwater Company's headquarters and are cut off by the road from the rest of the canal and the Upper Lock.

Therefore our first access onto the Thames & Severn Canal towpath is off the Old Bath Road bridge at Wallbridge. From this point all the way up to the Sapperton tunnel entrance the towpath, or its replacement, is public right of way and gives a continuous canal walk of some seven-and-a-half miles. The bridge crosses the tail of the Upper Lock and to the left by the side of the Bell Inn are one pair of the entrance gate-pillars to the Thames & Severn wharf, a site now occupied by Graham Reeves builders' merchants. From the stone parapets of this bridge can be seen the Upper Lock and from the opposite side of the road the canal bed is seen swinging round towards the Lower Lock and the junction across the road, but this length is not a public right of way.

Once on the towpath a look under the bridge shows that it has been widened for increased road traffic and ahead are the almost complete bottom gates of the lock in their closed position. These gates are the best remaining examples anywhere along the canal but of course they are in no way serviceable and are probably in excess of seventy years old. The wide lock chamber was built to take Severn trows as were all the locks up to and just beyond Brimscombe. It is crossed by an iron girder bridge leading into the former Midland Railway yards alongside the canal, and built incidentally on the Canal Company's land. The story of relationships with railway companies is extremely complex, and as much involved with rivalry between the various railway projects of the day as with canal-railway competition. Attempts to convert the canal into a railway were made in the mid-1880s, and the Midland's extension of its

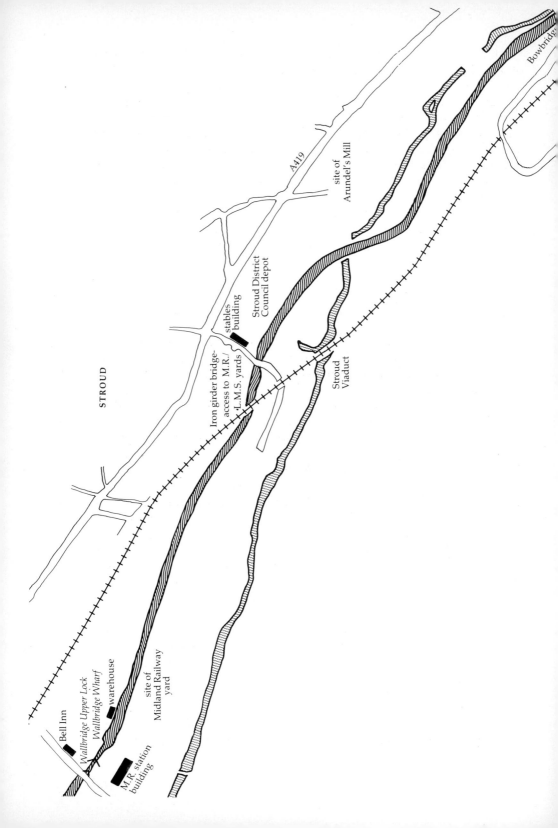

STROUD

Bell Inn

Wallbridge Upper Lock

Wallbridge Wharf

warehouse

site of
Midland Railway
yard

M.R. station
building

Iron girder bridge-
access to M.R./
L.M.S. yards

stables
building

Stroud District
Council depot

Stroud
Viaduct

A419

site of
Arundel's Mill

Bowbridge

Stonehouse and Nailsworth branch into Stroud in 1882 is part of that story. The wooden station building, the goods shed and the track bed are still there but the rails have long since been taken up. However, the bridge and its approaches make a good vantage point from which to look down at the wharf and the lock.

Across the top of the lock chamber a large strong dam has been built and it holds back the correct depth of water for a considerable distance up the canal. This section looks to be navigable and is used for fishing by a local club, especially opposite the area of the wharf where special wooden landing places have been built out from the towpath.

Stone blocks edge the towpath here and across the canal the stone warehouse erected in 1828 when it was clear that the Stroud wharf was second only to Brimscombe in the Company's earning power. It survives albeit with a modern storage building added. At this point there was a large wooden crane on the wharfside for loading and unloading barges, as this wharf did business in direct competition to the wharf of the Stroudwater Navigation just a few hundred yards away down the canal.

The canal now stretches away for about half-a-mile towards the lofty red brick arches of the Stroud viaduct where the Great Western Railway crossed the canal on a girder bridge built in 1844. Originally the viaduct was supported on wooden beams in common with early G.W.R. building practice but it was later clad with bricks. At this point a short length of the canal has become a casualty of the new (1987/88) Stroud east/west bypass which cuts through the canal bed under the viaduct and sweeps back up towards the A419. By lengthy negotiations the Canal Trust achieved a diversion of the canal line to pass beneath the new road by the provision of an underpass bridge.

Almost immediately beyond the viaduct is a small girder access bridge across the canal into the old Midland Railway yards over to the right. In 1923 this company became part of the L.M.S. Railway, and by walking up the track from this bridge it is possible to see within the Stroud District Council depot the remains of a long two-storeyed building which was the stables for the L.M.S. carriers' horses. In this building the horses went 'up stairs' to bed down as the stables were over the hay and cart sheds.

It is also by means of this bridge that the towpath now winds up and over the canal making its first changeover from the right hand to the left hand side. The towpath is a good firm pathway and appears to be well used and it is difficult to realise in this location that we are still only just half a mile from the centre of Stroud.

After a short distance we come on the left to the site of Arundel's Mill and a saw mill both of which made use of the considerable power to be obtained from the River Frome at this point. With the mills eventually

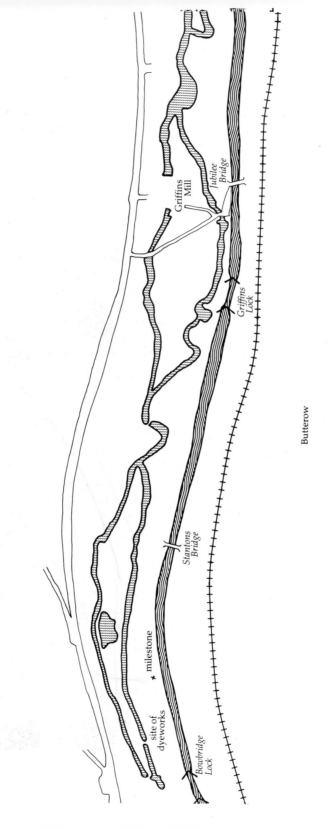

Butterow

Griffins
Mill

Jubilee
Bridge

Griffins
Lock

Stantons
Bridge

milestone

site of
dyeworks

Bowbridge
Lock

now lack their cast iron plates, some removed in earlier years for safe-keeping and never restored, and some (regrettably) stolen in recent years as souvenirs. Old photographs show that the Bowbridge stone was well sited to be used as a mooring post for the wharf here.

Access: from the Stroud-Cirencester road, turn off at the British Oak Inn on the Rodborough road and after about 100 yards this road crosses the canal at Bowbridge lock.

Bowbridge Lock to Bagpath Bridge

Beyond Bowbridge the canal curves gently round towards Stantons Bridge which gave access across the canal between the communities on the valley slope and the mills in the valley bottom. There is a good deal of water in this reconstructed and rewatered section which was dredged during 1975 when repairs were also made to Stantons Bridge. The stretch of water is now fished by the Stroud and District Angling Club.

Within a straight quarter of a mile the canal comes to Griffins Lock, which marks the end of the half mile re-watered section up from Bowbridge, and the walker will now become more aware of the valley in which the canal is situated. The surviving buildings of many former woollen mills stand on the river Frome over to the left; the valley sides slope steeply particularly up to the right to Butterow and Rodborough Common; here too the now ever present railway accompanies our progress up the valley. The towpath is well used and is pleasant easy walking leaving the town of Stroud well behind, becoming even more rural in outlook, with this length particularly well liked by swans and other waterbirds. A great deal of major clearance work and dredging was carried out here at Griffins Lock and on towards Ham Mill Lock by the Trust during 1975-6, even to the extent of making new top lock gates, but work here was discontinued partly as the result of a boundary dispute and the whole situation remains in abeyance. Although these locks remain derelict at least further deterioration has been arrested and perhaps some programme of work can be re-established here in years to come. A concrete block weir is now built across the top gate position in an attempt to retain water in the section up to Ham Mill Lock and so restrict the growth of weeds in the canal.

This is a good point to comment upon the advantages of retaining some water in the canal bed. The use of temporary weirs at the head of locks is already apparent as we follow the route and other examples will be noted. Apart from control of weed growth, weirs have some beneficial effect upon the otherwise uncontrolled flow of water through derelict locks and thus ensure a measure of conservation of deteriorating brickwork etc. We have already noted the visual attractiveness of a rewatered section and this is to be compared with other dry and neglected areas futher up the line. Full commercial rates for restoration are roughly £50,000 per lock and £50–75,000 per mile of canal. By utilizing volunteer and no-cost labour the Trust and other restoration groups can bring these frighteningly high figures down to about £5–10,000 per lock and £5–7,000 per mile of canal for uncomplicated sections. Thus we can appreciate the increasing value to the overall project of relatively simple conservation measures such as weir building, stonework repair etc.

Above Griffins Lock there is a small footbridge of lattice iron work on stone pillars known as Jubilee Bridge. Again it served to link the communities on either side of the canal or more particularly the Griffin's Mill workers with their work. The mill is now occupied by Batricar Ltd. making powered invalid cars, but like most of the other mills in this valley it has had a varied manufacturing career including the production of wooden parts for aircraft during the two world wars. Adjacent to the mill the towpath is edged with stone blocks to form a small wharf from which coal and other goods could be loaded and unloaded directly across one field and into the mill. It is believed that Jubilee Bridge was installed at the time of the Golden Jubilee of Queen Victoria in 1887 (another source dates it to be 1903). It replaced a temporary bridge which had itself been built in 1842 to restore the right of way after the collapse of the original bridge through neglect. In turn, the state of the bridge had become something of a sore point locally and demands were made for a replacement to restore the right of way. Jubilee Bridge has itself been restored and painted by the Trust.

From here the canal proceeds in a straight line towards Ham Mill Lock and Bridge which takes its name from a woollen mill adjacent to the canal. The mill is now occupied by Carpets of Worth and still retains a small link with its old 'woollen' days. An interesting point to make here is that the last working barge load of coal on the Thames & Severn Canal was brought up here to Ham Mill in 1933 in the barge *Dorothy* owned by E.T. Ward & Sons Ltd., carriers of Stroud. The barge tied up just above Ham Mill and was unloaded straight into the mill. Now there is another concrete block weir built across the position of the top gates here and some deeply worn tow-rope grooves cut into the underside of the arch of the bridge. A short distance above this lock is an accommodation bridge called Bagpath Bridge which has been extensively rebuilt by a small team of Trust members with new work on the parapets and abutments in 1978-9. This gave access across the canal to the former Thrupp Mill and village. It was in a foundry established on this site in the 1830s – the Phoenix Iron Works – that John Ferrabee established a reputation for the manufacture of textile machinery and lawn mowers, an early example of which is preserved in Stroud Museum. The site is

now covered by modern factory buildings of Hawker Siddeley Power Plant Ltd.

Bagpath Bridge to Bourne Lock

From Bagpath Bridge the canal curves gently to the south-east towards Hope Mill Lock or Ridlers Lock, which lies alongside the site of the old Hope Mill. Largely rebuilt early in the nineteenth century, this was used as a silk mill and is thought to be the last of this type of mill to operate in the Stroud valley. The lock has now been filled and an access road comes into the area now occupied by Air Plants Ltd. This development now creates one of the major obstacles to the restoration of the canal and will probably involve a diversion.

It was just above this lock that an enterprising private boat building yard grew up and thrived for many years. It was initially set up by Edwin Clark & Co. in 1878 but was later taken over by Abdela & Mitchell Ltd., in 1899. All types of boats were built ranging from small sailing

20. Griffins Lock in 1896 looking down to Stantons Bridge. One of a number of views photographed along the Thames & Severn that year.

111

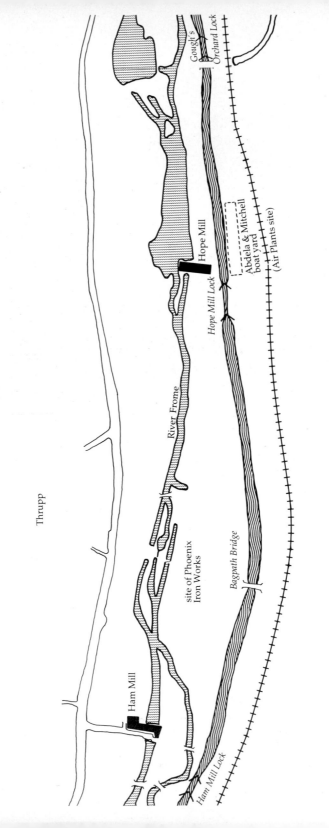

Thrupp

Gough's
Orchard Lock

Hope Mill

Hope Mill Lock

Abdela & Mitchell
boat yard

(Air Plants site)

River Frome

site of Phoenix
Iron Works

Bagpath Bridge

Ham Mill

Ham Mill Lock

boats to large steam screw and paddle river launches, many for use in South America. The yard continued building until 1934, using the canal to get its boats out, but following the official abandonment of the canal in 1933 it became necessary to use road transport, with boats often in pieces for assembly elsewhere, and the yard finally ceased activity just prior to the Second World War. The yard had both open and covered slipways launching its boats at an angle into the canal just above the lock and the old mill buildings on the towpath side of the canal were used as offices and as the boiler and engine factory. An excellent photographic record exists of most of the craft built there and of the yard, the building and the workforce (see Further Reading). Several of the vessels built at this yard are known to survive in various parts of the country. In amongst the new buildings on the site can be seen one of the old boat-building sheds angled to the canal and at the rear a long line of open sheds of a similar date.

In about another quarter of a mile we arrive at Goughs Orchard Lock just alongside the once-extensive Brimscombe Mills. The lock has been known by several names locally, reflecting the owners and lessees of the mill buildings; Dalloway's recalls the family who occupied the mills at

21. Unloading coal into Brimscombe Mills from the narrow boat 'Alert' at Goughs Orchard Lock before the First World War. A.M. Pearce of Brimscombe was a well-known haulier on the Thames & Severn.

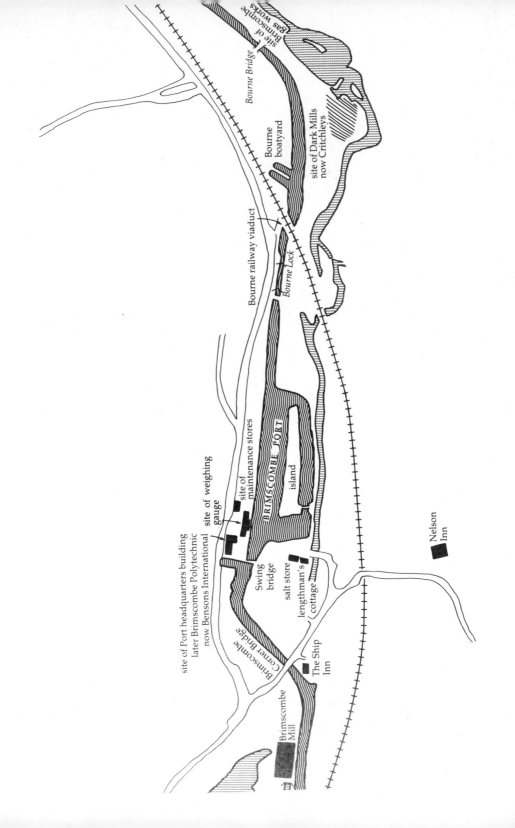

the time the canal was constructed; Lewis the subsequent miller, and Evans the well-established firm of P.C. Evans & Sons which had 124 looms at work there in 1889. Subsequent amalgamations led to closure and eventually to demolition and only parts now remain. Of the lock itself, partial infilling is rather unsightly but from here into Brimscombe the canal has been infilled and covered over. When the canal was operational we would now be almost in sight of the great inland port at Brimscombe as the towpath comes alongside an old public house called The Ship. The inn has a good painted sign showing its associations with the canal and one or two old photographs may be seen at the bar. It is the first genuine canalside public house since leaving Stroud two-and-a-half miles away and together with two other public houses now closed – the Nelson and the Port – it served the needs of the employees at the port and the bargees who were held up there for the loading and unloading of cargoes. The Ship makes an excellent stopping place for refreshments along this stretch.

Access point : from Stroud-Cirencester road A419 alongside; bus service.

The towpath now leaves its original line, caused by some severe road reconstruction and redirection of the River Frome at Brimscombe corner; here a substantial bridge once spanned the canal and allowed the towpath to change sides for the approach to the Port. In order to get back onto the line of the canal it is necessary to follow the road uphill past The Ship, alongside Port Mill which appears to be one of the best-maintained mills along the whole valley with lawns and seats alongside its mill pond, and to turn left at the fingerpost PORT FOUNDRY into the car-park of Bensons International Systems Ltd. This car park approximately represents the large area which once was Brimscombe Port, and nowadays it is difficult to imagine what a hive of activity this area must once have been on the canal.

Brimscombe Port

The Port was the focal point of the life of the Thames & Severn. It was the headquarters and early meeting place of the proprietors of the Canal Company with a staff of upwards of seventeen clerks, apprentices, wharfmen, labourers and craftsmen. This activity can be appreciated from a glance at the 1826 scene at Brimscombe reproduced as plate 23. The significance of the Port was, of course, its function as a tranship-ment point between Severn trows and Thames barges; the locks this far east from Stroud were built to a different gauge than those onwards from Brimscombe, the result not necessarily of bad planning but very typical of the approach adopted by canal promoters and proprietors of

the day. Although transhipment at Brimscombe Port may not have been planned by the Company purely as a means of income, it did of course yield port dues and compromise on gauge in this way offended neither the Severn nor the Thames interests backing the canal. It meant delay both to the trader and the sender of goods.

Basically the Port consisted of a large basin, about 700' long and 250' wide which a nineteenth century commentator estimated could hold a hundred vessels. The plan shows the layout: a central island storage area for coal and other goods susceptible to theft, and on the northern side the principal wharf with its main building. This was a remarkable structure containing warehouse, office and agents house in three stories; the records show that this was built by Thomas Cook from Painswick who was by trade a master mason, but who became a considerable building contractor in the area. He had various contracts on the canal during its building period and also – incidentally – was responsible for the rebuilding works at Gloucester Gaol during the same decade. Cook built the Port warehouse between 1786-9 and the proprietors first met there the following year.

Also on this side of the wharf was a transit shed, a forge and later a boat-weighing machine. It is a great pity that none of this now survives, especially the wharfhouse which would almost certainly have been the ideal base from which to launch the revival of interest in the canals across the Cotswolds. This revival did not come early enough to save

22. Approaching Brimscombe Port with the wharfhouse building in the background. This postcard view was taken from Brimscombe Bridge, now demolished and levelled.

BRIMSCOMBE PORT

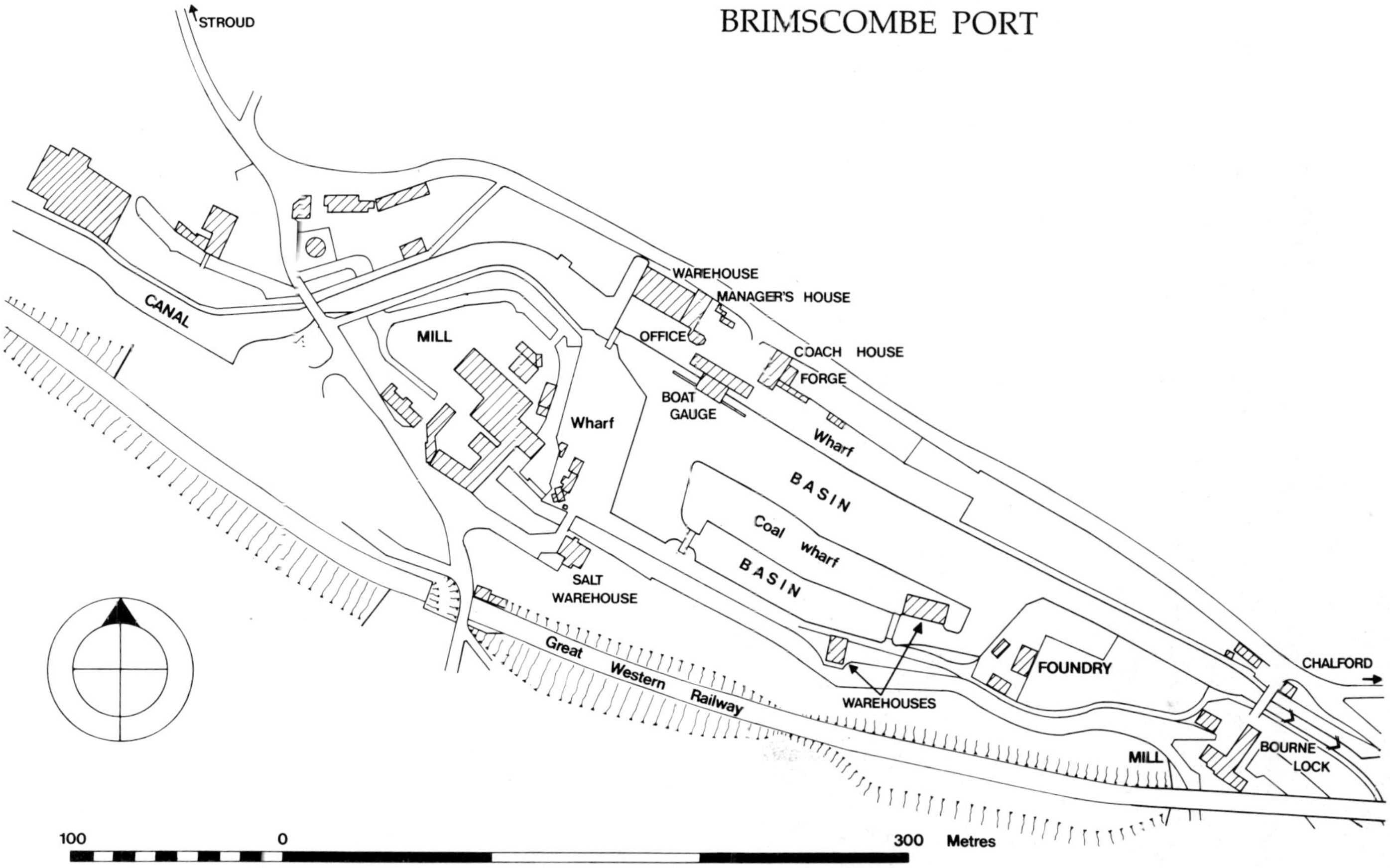

STROUD

CANAL

MILL

Wharf

WAREHOUSE

MANAGER'S HOUSE

OFFICE

COACH HOUSE

BOAT GAUGE

FORGE

Wharf

SALT WAREHOUSE

B A S I N

Coal Wharf

B A S I N

WAREHOUSES

FOUNDRY

Great Western Railway

CHALFORD

BOURNE LOCK

MILL

Metres

100   0   300

117

these buildings which were cleared away in 1964 for the modern factory development now covering the site. The basin itself had already been filled in years before and now forms the car park for Bensons'; the Company generously allows access to interested visitors into the wharf area where a plaque on the office wall gives a brief history of the site, and a (?replica) mileage plate records WALBRIDGE 2½ INGLESHAM 26¼.

Following the takeover of the canal by the Gloucestershire County Council in 1900 the main warehouse was partly converted into a Polytechnic School in 1905 and then fully converted and officially opened in 1911. It became the Brimscombe Secondary Modern School under the Education Act of 1944 and finally moved to Eastcombe Manor School in 1962, following which the buildings were finally demolished.

Very little remains of the other Port buildings. A lengthman's cottage has been demolished since the first edition of the Guide but the small adjoining salt store survives at the southern entrance to the car park. It has recently been surveyed (note the ventilation slits in the upper walls). Its future too must be in some doubt. Everything else about the Port must be left to the imagination and the host of good photographs that record the Port throughout the latter part of its life. From a restoration point of view it is hoped that the bed of the River Frome can be used to get round this major obstacle.

Before leaving this area, note again the impressive buildings of Port

23. Brimscombe Port — a scene of busy activity in 1826. The wharfhouse, transit shed and port-side cranes can clearly be seen — all now obliterated.

Mill, most of which are late nineteenth century in date; the history of this mill is inextricably bound up with that of the other mill buildings in Brimscombe we have already seen. To continue along the canal, we must now follow the path alongside the river Frome passing the Port Foundry buildings and gaining access to the towpath again at Bourne Lock. This was a hybrid lock built to the dimensions 90' length and 16' 1" width – the length to accommodate Thames barges and the width to allow Severn trows to gain access to the Company's boat yard a little to the east, virtually all trace of which has now sadly disappeared. Alongside the lock stands Bourne Mill, still the home of a number of small businesses – notice particularly the painted sign on the upper floor for 'H.S. Hack Ltd., Stick Manufacturers, Bourne Mill'. Both the buildings here are excellent examples of the great phase of mill rebuilding in the period 1825-50 when the woollen cloth industry was at its height.

24. The basin at Brimscombe Port c. 1907 — a postcard view looking towards Port Mills with the salt store and cottage in front.

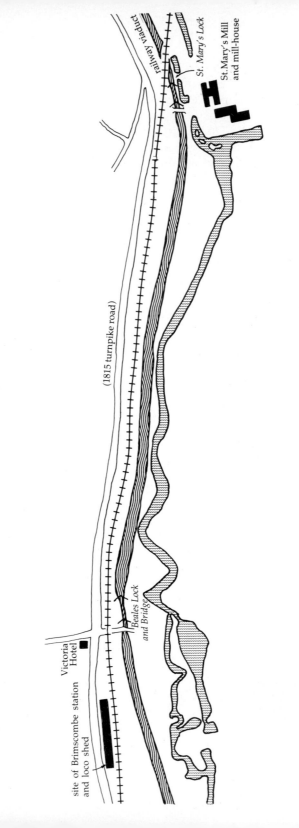

site of Brimscombe station
and loco shed

Victoria
Hotel

Beales Lock
and Bridge

(1815 turnpike road)

railway viaduct

St. Mary's Lock

St. Mary's Mill
and mill-house

CHAPTER TEN

Brimscombe to Golden Valley

Bourne Lock to Chalford Wharf

Above Bourne Lock the railway swings back across both valley and canal on a small low brick arched viaduct, but the iron girder span over the canal has been underfilled and water is now channelled through pipes and the towpath diverted through an Armco tube. On the right the site of Dark Mills is now Critchley Bros. plastics factory which has been here since 1906; the present buildings are the third rebuilding here.

Across the canal on the left the scant remains of the Thames & Severn Canal Company boatyard could just be identified until recently. This yard was set up soon after the canal was opened, and was the scene of much boat-building and repairing activity. Humphrey Household tells us of the work at the yard, the construction of both the Thames barge and the Severn type of vessel and the upkeep of the fleet of over fifty vessels which the Company maintained during the period when it also acted as a carrying company. Conditions were fairly simple; boats were constructed in the open in the later of the two dry docks or on the bank of the canal from where they were launched sideways into the cut. Most of the site has now been engulfed by the expansion of the Olympic Varnish Co.

The canal has now gently curved west/east and within the narrow confines of the floor of the valley it is very interesting to note that the road, railway, canal and river are all within a few yards of each other. By the now levelled site of Bourne Bridge stood Brimscombe Gas Works to which coal was brought direct by canal barge. The site is now used by Watersmeet Garage for the repair of commercial vehicles etc and only the keen eye can detect any historical significance for the various buildings.

Alongside the fence to Critchley's factory there is a good example of a milepost – three miles from Wallbridge – before we reach Beales Lock and Bridge. The towpath does not pass under this bridge and must have been a nuisance to the bargees as they would have had to unhitch their towrope to pass. From the main road there is good access from the Victoria Hotel down to this bridge by means of a footpath crossing the railway line at the site of Brimscombe station, of which absolutely

nothing appears to remain. Beales Lock is in good condition and the strong dam built across the top holds back a good depth of water in the next half-mile section up to St. Marys Lock. In the days of steam engines on the railway, the water level in the canal above Beales Lock had to be kept to the correct depth as it was used to supply water to the three banker engines stationed at Brimscombe to provide assistance to the trains up the long bank to Sapperton tunnel – a splendid memory to both the eye and ear of many railway enthusiasts! Even after abandonment of the canal in 1933 this arrangement still applied and is now one of the reasons why this stretch of canal and the dam remain in such good repair. This length must represent one of the most attractive sections of canal along the valley.

St. Marys Mill with the mill-house behind now come into view on the right and remain one of the finest groups of mill-buildings in the valley. Both the water wheel and a Tangye Compound Steam Engine survive intact, both having been restored by Mr. Reynolds who lives in St. Marys House. There is also a portable boiler which can be used to steam the engine. Until 1980 walking sticks were still being made at this mill but following a disastrous fire production has been moved to a mill in the Nailsworth valley. St. Marys Mill House has associations with two eighteenth century Astronomers Royal and it is believed with Roger Bacon, the thirteenth century discoverer of gunpowder. Just before St. Marys Lock is one of the few places where there is direct level

25. The 'Humaytha', one of the products of the boat-building yard of Abdela & Mitchell at Hope Mill, Brimscombe. Many were for use abroad, the 'Humaytha' in Brazil. c. 1905.

connection between the canal and river by means of a culvert under the towpath, and this is therefore another reason for the good water levels in the canal along this length. The lock chamber is in good condition but once again the railway comes back across the canal, the original bridge has been underfilled and the canal is culverted into a pipe creating another obstacle to restoration. The towpath is also diverted into a separate tube.

From this point the locks come closer together as the canal climbs up the valley and once through the footway it is only a short distance to Iles or Grist Mill Lock which has remnants of its gates remaining in position. On the left hand side just before the lock is Clayfield's Mill, now converted into cottages; part of this site was cleared for road-widening in the mid-1960s. A small stream which comes down out of the valley side powered a waterwheel in the mill and then entered the canal. Looking at the parapets of the bridges leading up to the road along this section, the additions in stone and brick become obvious where the tracks were sloped up to the new turnpike road built in 1815. Previously, these bridges were merely humpbacked over the canal. The site of Iles Mill was over to the right hand side of the towpath between the canal

26. Beales Lock and bridge in 1957 with the now vanished Brimscombe station in the background. Looking west.

and railway line but it was gutted by fire in 1913 and now all that remains is the house and a few odd buildings. Its other name derives from the Grist family who made flock and shoddy there a century ago.

Within one hundred yards we come to the site of Ballingers Lock. The infilled chamber is now covered by a small row of three garages with the canal culverted into a pipe beneath. At the far end notice some sluice gear and the water disappearing through a grating under the garages.

Access: There is good access from the road at this point as it comes very close to the canal.

We might also note how the road-widening has taken its toll of the canal line. The towpath boundary wall is in reasonably good condition all along this section, which formed part of a 'Stroud Valley Facelift' project in the mid-1960s.

Chalford Wharf and roundhouse are now in sight and we can see the stone blocks edging the towpath which formed the wharf; some still have iron mooring rings fixed to them. Chalford wharf was a busy place with so many mills both large and small in fairly close proximity, and the canal widened out at this point to form a 'winding hole' or turning place for barges. This is as good a reminder as any of one of the major problems which the Canal Company faced throughout its life; much of its trade was concentrated in the western section, and only a relatively

27. Looking east towards Chalford Chapel c. 1910. This section between St. Mary's and Grist Mill Locks with Clayfield's Mill on the left.

small amount actually traversed the entire length of the Thames & Severn. Lucrative as this local western trade might be (particularly in coal carrying), the heavy maintenance costs of the long climb to the summit, the summit itself and the whole of the eastern section were offset by relatively meagre returns. When the other imbalance – a far greater movement eastwards of traffic than ever flowed westwards – is added, we have some idea of the basic miscalculation of traffic flow which affected the financial well-being of the canal through much of its life.

The most outstanding feature at Chalford is the roundhouse, the first of five such buildings we will be seeing along the canal. Other comments about the type will follow later, but we should note here that these roundhouses were built about 1790-1 as lengthmen's or watchmen's cottages. Each had three storeys, the ground floor for a stable (entering here from the road) with the first and the second floors as living accommodation. Note that access from the canalside led into the first floor. Each was built in stone and rendered with stucco, although the Chalford building has recently had its stucco removed during conversion to a *private house*. It has in fact had a very interesting history

28. *Postcard view of Ballingers Lock c. 1904 with Chalford wharf beyond. Garages now stand on this site.*

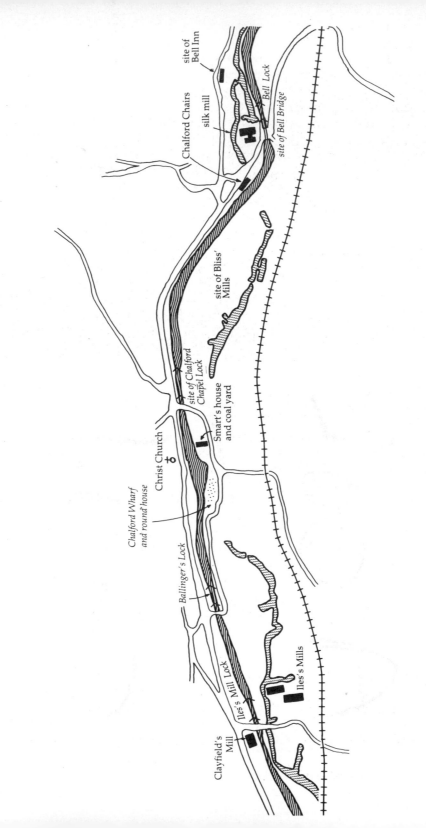

site of Bell Inn

Chalford Chairs

silk mill

Bell Lock

site of Bell Bridge

site of Bliss' Mills

site of Chalford Chapel Lock

Smart's house and coal yard

Christ Church

Chalford Wharf and round'house

Ballinger's Lock

Iles's Mill Lock

Iles's Mills

Clayfield's Mill

ever since the canal closed, being for some years a small museum housing a private collection of Thames & Severn memorabilia and artefacts.

Other elements of the wharf should be noted before we move on; the pillars at the entrance from the road remain in situ, and nearby is the overflow weir which still carries surplus water into the river Frome. The landscaping of the wharf is obvious, part of the Gloucestershire County Council project to create an amenity area. This seems to have worn fairly well, and prominently displayed is some of the sluice gear from Sevill's mill. Across the road stands the former Company's Arms Inn, which as Chalford Place dates back in part to the fifteenth century (it has for example an upper hall of that date). Derelict for some years, the building has recently been restored with some care and remains a private house. However, it is possible to admire the very fine (and typically Cotswold) gables added to the north side of the building by the seventeenth century.

Chalford Wharf to Valley Lock

The first house facing you as you leave Chalford Wharf belonged to James Smart, bargemaster and coal merchant. His firm had its own fleet of barges trading on the canals and faded lettering on the north wall of the house still advertises this fact (what about restoring this, I wonder?).

29. Chalford wharf in April 1937 with repairs in progress on the round-house. Chapel Lock just beyond the bridge.

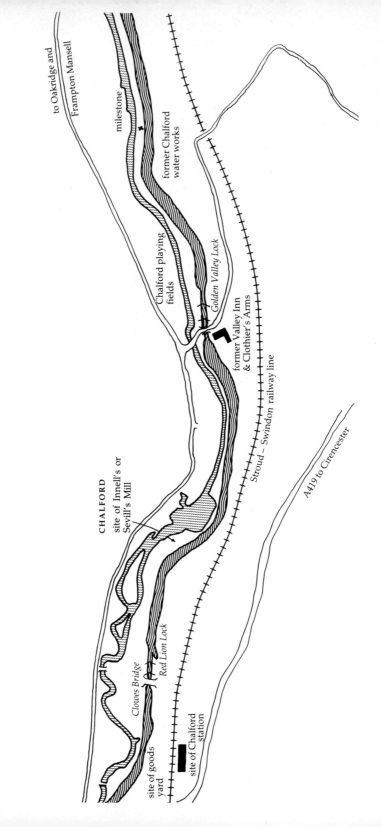

to Oakridge and
Frampton Mansell

milestone

former Chalford
water works

Chalford playing
fields

Golden Valley Lock

former Valley Inn
& Clothier's Arms

Stroud – Swindon railway line

A419 to Cirencester

CHALFORD

site of Innell's or
Sevill's Mill

Clowes Bridge

Red Lion Lock

site of goods
yard

site of Chalford
station

The site is still a coal yard, although road transport has long since brought coal up from the railway at Stroud. Across the road is Chalford Church which gave its name to the lock when it was a chapel of ease, and it is up to this point that the western section of the canal remained at its most active even in some small way with Smarts barges trading right up to abandonment in 1933. There was another small yard known as Whitings Coal Yard just above Chalford Chapel Lock.

The canal leaves Chalford in a culverted pipe following infilling of Chapel lock in 1964 for road widening and improvements. Built into the culvert arch is the milestone and plate WALBRIDGE 4 INGLESHAM 24¾ from this part of the canal. Crossing the road, the towpath line follows behind the bus shelter and for the next section road widening has taken about half of the canal bed. Behind the stone wall on the right was the group of buildings known as Bliss' Mill; there were in fact once five separate mill concerns here employing at their peak in excess of one thousand people in the manufacture of walking sticks etc., the majority of which were exported world-wide. The site now forms the Chalford trading estate and some of the older buildings survive amongst modern additions.

30. Chalford roundhouse in 1947 with the Company's Arms behind.

129

The canal now winds past the last group of mill buildings in this more industrialised part of the route passing the modern canal-side works of Chalford Chairs, a woodworking mill for many years, and approaching the crossing of the main A419 Stroud-Cirencester road. Here the substantial Bell Bridge was built in stone in 1815 to carry the new turnpike road over the canal. It too has fallen victim to road improvements and we must cross the road noting that the river Frome is culverted deep under the canal here.

Access: this is a good access point for this area and indeed for the section right up to Daneway. Some limited parking.

Across the road the canal turns away from the road line up Cowcombe hill and the towpath changes over to the left-hand side. On the left an old brick silk mill (now Arnolds Designs) has a significance in the later years of the Arts & Crafts movement in Gloucestershire. It was taken over by Peter de Waals, foreman to the Barnsley brothers, furniture makers at Daneway house. Following the break-up of the group of craftsmen at Daneway, Peter de Waals brought the workforce to this mill and carried on their traditional type of furniture-making until just before the Second World War.

Most of the chamber of Bell Lock remains; this was one of the most photographed locks along this stretch of canal in Edwardian times. Up to the right above the high retaining wall stood Chalford railway station and goods yards built in 1897, but this has all been swept away with almost no trace remaining of this busy little place. Bell Lock and Red Lion Lock are close together and take their names from nearby public houses. Both were reached by small footbridges across the River Frome on the left hand side; the Bell has disappeared completely although the Red Lion remains and makes a good place to stop for refreshments.

We are now four and a half miles from Wallbridge, and Red Lion Lock is significant in the history of the Thames & Severn in several ways. The original cutting of the line of the canal was advanced from west to east and had reached this point by the autumn or early winter of 1784, about eighteen months after the commencement of works. It enabled access to be gained to the 'Black Gutter', the local name for a group of springs in the valley side which were harnessed for canal use; hence we can assume that these and other sources were already 'in commission' when the first vessel is reported to have entered the locks at Wallbridge in January 1785. This significance is supported by the construction of a fine example of a stone bridge across the tail of the lock with its keystone inscribed 'CLOWS ENGr 1785'. Josiah Clowes was the Canal Company's 'surveyor, engineer and head carpenter' from 1783 and effectively the resident engineer putting Whitworth's proposals into effect on the ground. As he was very much in charge of the construction programme, it is not surprising to find this permanent record at Red Lion Lock. In fact, there is another, as the mason Herbert Stansfield had his own name and the date 4 December 1784 carved on the lock chamber – how interesting it would be if each lock bore such a useful record! Certainly, the stone bridge has a character of its own which we will not see elsewhere on the canal, although the stone bridges at Whitehall and Tarlton Road also deserve special mention.

Alongside the lock the milestone shows well, and its plate has been preserved in Stroud Museum. The towpath is good in this section and indeed well used. The railway line is still climbing up the valley alongside the canal and the steep gradient on the line is certainly noticeable when a hardworking train comes up the valley. Events were much more dramatic in the days of steam when heavy firing produced lots of smoke and noise from both the lead engine and the banker engine at the rear. The canal and railway now both curve round past the now demolished woollen and silk mill known as Innell's or Sevill's Mill. These deviations were necessary to avoid the mill pond within the

31. Bell Lock c. 1910 from a Frith & Co. postcard view. The lock-gates had been replaced in 1904. Bell Inn and Red Lion Inn both visible.

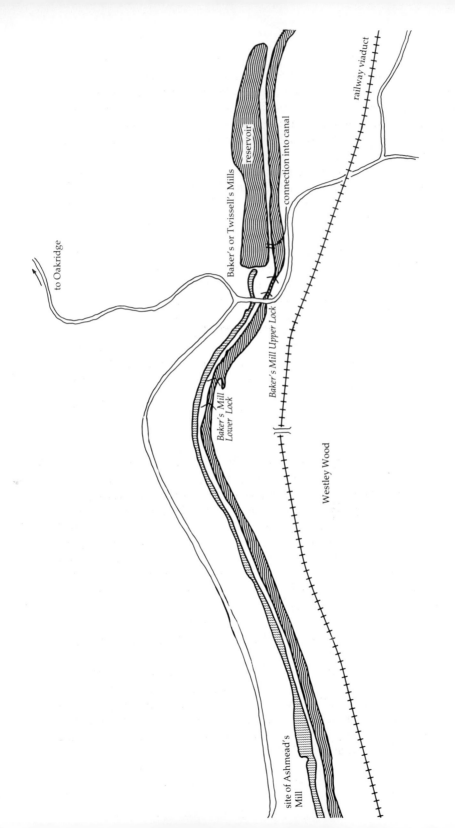

to Oakridge

reservoir

Baker's or Twissell's Mills

connection into canal

Baker's Mill Upper Lock

Baker's Mill Lower Lock

site of Ashmead's Mill

Westley Wood

railway viaduct

narrow confines of the valley and discussions with the mill-owners caused a six-month delay in the construction programme in 1785. The mill site is now a small factory making cardboard boxes and gaskets and the only remnant of the mill is a long building, now three houses, which was originally a mill shed away from but parallel to the canal. There is a stone edge to the towpath here where barges once tied up to bring coal and supplies to the mill.

Around the bend we soon come to Valley Lock, which together with the previous two locks has raised the canal through 26' in just half a mile. The records reveal that this lock was built by George Makin for the sum of £48. 11s. 0d., roughly the cost quoted for several other locks along the line. The wooden bridge across the lock has now been replaced by a concrete structure and this leads almost immediately to a fine Cotswold house, now a *private residence* but formerly the Valley Inn. Originally it was a mill-house and its first name as a pub was the Clothiers Arms. Lettering on the wall facing the canal still shows faintly. Below the lock was a saw mill on the river, of which only the grooves cut by its water wheel in the stonework of the sluices can still be seen.

From here the canal leaves the village of Chalford and the next section has a character all its own for the two and a quarter miles to Daneway; the line and the Frome follow each other all along the valley and the scene appears almost unchanged in the two centuries since the canal was built.

Valley Lock to Puck Mill Upper Lock

Above Valley Lock the towpath is shaded by a line of overhanging trees, which contribute to the peaceful woodland atmosphere of the right-hand bank of the canal. In due course a large brick building comes into view on the right. This was the original Chalford Water Works built in the 1880s and is a typical pump-house with round-headed iron-framed windows. Coal supplies were delivered by canal for the steam-driven pumps. A photograph reproduced in Humphrey Household's history shows these buildings with the County Council's steam dredger *Empress* at work earlier this century. The building is now used for car restoration and a small sign summarises its history.

Another milepost is prominent near here; over in the fields to the left are a house and a few remains of Ashmeads mill which once processed silk but was demolished in 1903. The incidence we have noticed of silk mills in the valley shows that silk cloth production tended to take over from woollen cloth production when the latter was gradually lost to the larger Yorkshire mills which were prepared to modernise in order to remain competitive. It is probably fair to say that Stroud valley woollen mills were a little complacent about modernisation and so gradually lost their trade in a decreasing market.

There is now a straight stretch flanked on the bankside by Westley Wood, for about half a mile up to Bakers Mill Lower Lock also known as Boultings Lock. A dam across the top of the lock holds back water up to the next lock and it was the earlier Thames & Severn Canal Trust which was responsible in 1897 for lining this pound with concrete to stop water leakage. It became known locally as the 'conk' and was used as a huge swimming pool.

At Baker's Mill Upper Lock the lane along the valley from Chalford to Frampton Mansell crosses over the canal by a bridge now reinforced and perhaps less interesting than others along the line. Access from the road and very limited parking are available here, a wooden footbridge crossing the lock and recording, incidentally, the interest of the Gloucestershire Trust for Nature Conservation in the valley from this point upwards. At the lockside was a small wharf at which coal was unloaded for Oakridge silk mill.

Below the lock is the mill house and surviving buildings of Baker's or Twissell's mill, the latter name after a seventeenth century clothing family. It later became a corn mill. Immediately above the mill and covering the mill pond the Thames & Severn Canal Company bought land and constructed a large reservoir as a source of water to the locks lower down. This had become necessary because of the failure of the arrangements at Sapperton and particularly of a smaller reservoir at Daneway. The location was virtually the only place of sufficient size high enough up the valley to be of use as a reservoir, and therefore the Company was almost forced to buy this land and then to acquire Puck Mill just further up the canal (putting it out of business) in order to guarantee the water supply to fill the reservoir. This is almost 900' long, 94' wide and (should be) 6' deep with a capacity of more than $3\frac{1}{4}$ million gallons. The present lake is *private*, supports plenty of wildlife and occasionally is used for boating by the owners of the mill.

This whole area is very rural and peaceful with the wooded slopes of the valley coming down to the water's edge. The towpath runs between reservoir and canal as a raised path and in wet winter weather there can be a great deal of water on both sides. The connection between canal and reservoir is by means of a small culvert under the towpath just above Upper Lock. This section remains scenically one of the most interesting along the canal at any season of the year.

Once the canal clears the end of the reservoir the two locks at Puck Mill appear quite close together, and over to the right the Frampton Mansell railway viaduct crosses a small side valley with the village up above. The canal is usually quite dry here above the level of the reservoir and the top end of the Lower Lock was blocked off for use as a swimming pool some years ago. The pound between the Lower and Upper Locks was a constant worry to the Canal Company as it leaked

very badly, losing water almost as quickly as it received it. This pound was therefore the scene of a considerable reconstruction effort in 1907 by Gloucestershire County Council which had taken over the canal in 1900. Over a three-month period, the canal bed was completely stripped out and repuddled with clay in the traditional manner. A series of photographs survives of these activities and apart from minor details the scenes are probably no different from those a visitor to the original construction might have witnessed 120 years previously. In both cases, virtually the entire operation was undertaken by hand. This was the last of the large-scale work sites on the canal before it fell into disuse in the second decade of this century. No boats passed this way after 1911 with complete abandonment following in 1933.

At Puck Mill Upper Lock the towpath changes to the right hand side via a bridge at the tail of the lock. This is an interesting group, and the clever design can be studied here in some detail. The canal's construction obviously split up the limited farming land in the valley, hence the need for an 'accommodation' bridge to link up the severed portions; its siting immediately below the lock allows the farmer access on the level and the canal boats below sufficient headroom to pass before entering the lock, which rises here 8'. The lock gates were amongst the group replaced in 1902/3, and old photographs taken along the line of the canal in this period often show these dates incised on the new gates.

The whole of the Puck Mill area is indeed of interest. Close to the lock

32. Valley Lock looking west to Chalford c. 1910. Valley Inn alongside.

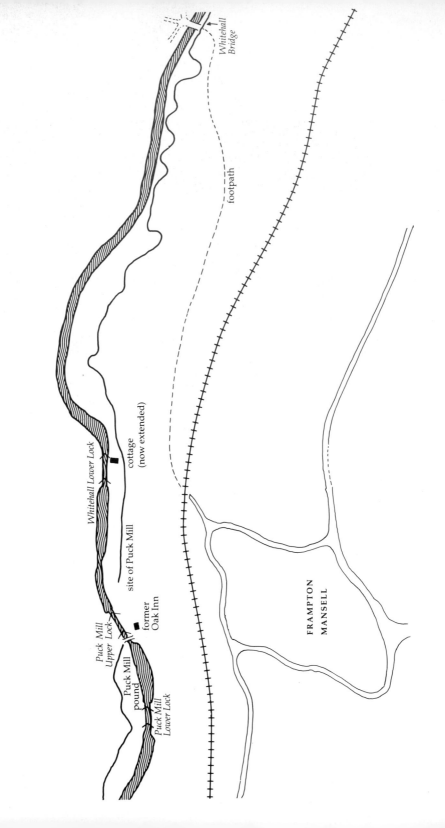

Whitehall Bridge

footpath

Whitehall Lower Lock

cottage
(now extended)

site of Puck Mill

Puck Mill
Upper Lock

former
Oak Inn

Puck Mill
pound

Puck Mill
Lower Lock

FRAMPTON
MANSELL

notice the barn which by its blocked-up windows etc. has clearly been used for another purpose. Indeed it has – it was once the Oak Inn, the only pub up the line between Chalford and Daneway. Its customers were almost totally derived from the canal. Nearby, there is hardly a trace of the four-storey Puck Mill with its cottage or two; only the burnt-out remains of the former mill-house just above the lock survive and this too has a doubtful future because of its present condition. Apart from the canal, the only other access to this area was down a track from Frampton Mansell. Recently the sale of much of this land has resulted in a new track being established along the line of a footpath from under the railway viaduct. Once over the bridge, please keep to the towpath line and avoid wandering off to the right onto *private property*. The re-development of this area in recent years from its former dereliction will be obvious, a welcome return of activity to this isolated spot.

33. Reconstruction teams at work at Puck Mill Lower Lock in 1907, the scene of considerable rebuilding by Gloucestershire County Council.

CHAPTER ELEVEN

Golden Valley to Sapperton Tunnel

Puck Mill to Daneway

For a section above the mill-site the canal seems to be pushed into the narrow valley, retained by the masonry walls of Puck Mill wharf. It soon opens out again as it approaches Whitehall Lower Lock. Here the chamber of the lock has been damaged by tree growth; a recent (and private) wooden bridge links both sides of the canal for the new owners of the lengthsman's cottage alongside the lock. After dereliction for some years, this simple rectangular building has been considerably modernised and enlarged recently – hence the new access road – and it is pleasing to see this building in use again. A Thames & Severn Canal

34. *Picturesque scene at Puck Mill before the reconstruction programme of 1907. Upper Lock in the foreground with the G.W.R. Frampton viaduct beyond. On the left the Oak Inn is just visible.*

property boundary stone has been rebuilt into the quoins of the property *(not accessible)*. The canal now swings round in an arc, leaving the stream and crossing the valley floor to the northern bank. The former mill pond for Puck Mill can only with great difficulty be recognised. From here to Daneway, a distance of almost a mile, there are no more houses in the valley.

The towpath is easily walked here although the canal bed is largely overgrown from the woods which tumble down the hillside on the far bank. The next feature is the brick and stone Whitehall Bridge, large and isolated in the valley floor. It too is an accommodation bridge, serving the rough tracks and footpaths which cross at this point. On the lower side a date stone has caused some interest; it reads 'W.D. 1784' – presumably the contractor-mason William Dennis, who was also responsible for work on two of the next group of locks up the line. Even so, the date 1784 seems early in the sequence of building the canal – perhaps this was the section worked on whilst the delay at Innell's mill delayed proceedings further down? Whitehall Bridge was the point selected as demarcation for the official abandonment of the canal to the

35. Samuel and Emily Elliott outside the Oak Inn at Puck Mill, alongside Upper Lock.

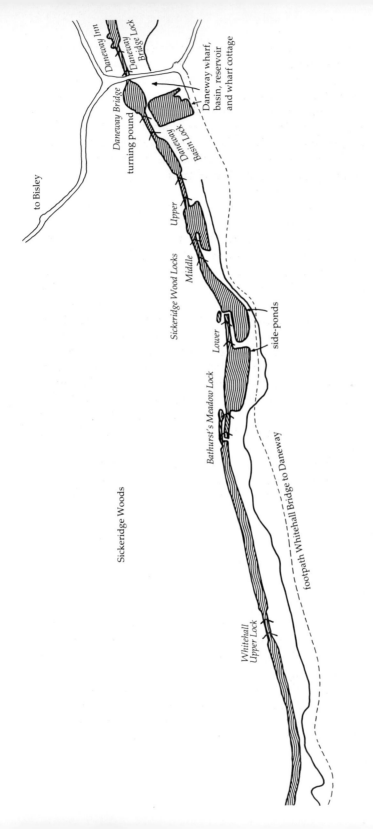

to Bisley

Sickeridge Woods

Daneway Inn

Daneway Lock
Bridge

Daneway Bridge

turning pound

Daneway wharf, basin, reservoir and wharf cottage

Daneway
Basin Lock

Upper

Middle

Sickeridge Wood Locks

Lower

Bathurst's Meadow Lock

side-ponds

footpath Whitehall Bridge to Daneway

Whitehall
Upper Lock

Sapperton railway tunnel

and has recently been exposed in the landscaping of the wharf area.

Following the towpath access is gained to Daneway Bridge from which most of the features of the wharf can be studied. This is *private property* and the small wharfingers cottage has been modernised and given a new lease of life in recent years; the wharf itself has been landscaped. There are two other good viewpoints for this area, one from the rough track that leads back down the valley to Whitehall Bridge from the opposite side of the wharf, and the second by walking a little way up the lane to Bisley from the road junction.

Across the bridge and on the top side of the lane stood a saw mill, originally water powered, but later converting to steam. There are no remains except a few stones from the sluice gear. The bridge and causeway across the valley at Daneway have recently been the centre of local controversy when the stability of the bank and bridge was found to need strengthening; the levelling down of both was only avoided by considerable local opposition, which led to a reprieve and the listing of the Daneway bridge (how many of the canal's bridges are protected in this way, I wonder?). Here again, involvement by the Trust helped preserve another feature on the canal line.

37. *The settlement at Daneway looking to Sapperton village on the skyline. Bridge, wharf and cottage in the foreground with the saw mill behind.*

143

east in 1927; the section we have been following from Wallbridge was not officially abandoned until 1933.

Sections of towpath in this area were kept clear for walkers by the local parish councils but in recent years a joint effort by the Canal Trust with other bodies has improved the line still more.

Incidentally, for railway buffs, a footpath heads up from here through the coppice on the south bank of the valley to cross the railway line just short of the entrance to the Sapperton tunnel; it is difficult to follow but eventually makes its way up to Frampton common on the minor road between that village and Sapperton.

Soon Whitehall Upper Lock is reached along a straight section and this lock can be considered as the bottom of a flight of seven locks all within the next half-mile up to the summit level at Daneway. We can get some idea of the amount of work involved in climbing this final section in a fully-laden barge, particularly as the records show just how difficult it was to maintain a good level of water in the pounds between the locks. In fact, there is a good case that the pounds – really reservoirs – were built too short to contain the amount of water required to fill each lock. In the final one and a half miles up the summit there are no less than twelve locks. One attempt – and a significant one – to reduce the quantities of water required can be seen in this group. A series of major improvements were carried out along the line of the canal following recommendations made in 1820, although it was not until 1841 that most of the locks in this section were shortened by about 20' with the insertion of a masonry arch across part of the lock chamber, the top gates being then rehung. Consumption was thus reduced by up to 20%. The original length of these locks (90'-93') was of course determined by the length of the Thames barges, but as most of the traffic was now carried by the shorter 70' narrow boats of the midland canals this improvement could be carried out without loss of trade.

Indeed, the need for water retention led also to the building of a series of side-ponds to the top five locks up to Daneway and these were probably all completed in 1823. At a depth of 3' and capable of holding up to 2,500 yards cubic capacity each, these ponds helped considerably in the constant battle against water loss. Their remains can still be made out amidst the undergrowth along this section – look particularly for the retaining bank on the right as we approach each lock in turn. They remain on *private property* so should only be studied from the towpath.

We next reach Bathurst Meadow Lock where the towpath again crosses over, now from the right to the left; the present wooden bridge is the successor to others in this position. None of this group of locks retains its gates although attempts have been made to hold back water with old railway sleepers etc. We are now in the steepest part of the valley and the locks are named after Sickeridge (or Siccaridge) Wood

which seems to hang above the walker coming up the towpath. Hence in quick succession, Sickeridge Wood Lower, Middle and Upper Locks, each rising 8' 5" with no more than 300 yards between them. The damage to the lock chambers from tree growth is obvious and restoration here will presumably involve rebuilding these locks in due course.

Daneway to Sapperton Tunnel

Daneway Basin Lock stands alongside the wharf and basin at Daneway. The valley at last opens out a little and this allowed just enough space for the wharf. At the top of the lock a small wooden footbridge, sadly now broken, gave access from towpath to wharf. Above the lock the canal opens out into an almost circular and stone edged turning pound with the wharf entrance off to the right; here boats moved to load or unload their cargoes which were mostly of coal, stone and timber. The basin was also used for barges to 'lay-up' whilst awaiting their turn to proceed and pass through the tunnel, navigation of which was strictly controlled on a four-hourly basis alternately each way both night and day. The basin also served as a reservoir supplying water to the flight of locks down the valley and we have already seen what was required when this proved to be inadequate. At some later date the basin was lined with concrete and this lining still remains in reasonable order

36. In the Golden Valley looking down to Bathurst Meadow Lock c. 1904.

The canal had been cut as far up as Daneway by the summer of 1786, nearly three years before the tunnel itself was completed. Thus this little hamlet became a hive of activity with the establishment of wharf, warehouse and coalyard, plus the construction of the road now running up the valley side to the village of Sapperton higher up. Hence goods could be carried by canal this far and transferred for road transport to Cirencester and beyond. Immediately beyond the bridge was Daneway Lock, where the canal reached the summit level. The total rise has been 241' from Wallbridge through twenty-eight locks. Again, the towpath changes sides, and the lock itself has been almost completely infilled to form a car park for the Daneway Inn alongside. This building too has canal significance for it was built by the canal contractor John Nock in 1784 as a base and accommodation for his men working on the construction of the tunnel just around the corner. It was sold out of the Canal Company's ownership in 1807 to become the Bricklayer's Arms inn and has been a public house ever since.

Access: Daneway is excellently placed to provide a base for canal exploration, refreshments en route, or – perhaps most useful of all –

38. Daneway Basin Lock where the canal reaches the summit level. Entrance to the basin on the left just above the lock.

one end of the Chalford-Daneway walk which is probably scenically the most interesting and certainly the most accessible of the entire canal length.

To approach the tunnel, follow the footpath sign 'Sapperton' from the bridge via a small stile into the field below the car park and this soon leads back to the towpath. Note: there is no right of way directly from car park to towpath. Across the field the line of the canal shows very well and the construction methods can be appreciated. The canal is cut into the slope of the hill and the spoil thrown up to form an embankment along which the towpath runs. The bed is quite deep as the summit level was intended to hold six feet of water and built to a greater width than lower down, both factors adding to its capacity as a reservoir. However, problems of leakage reduced the Company to a constant struggle to hold even four feet of water along the summit level.

Following the towpath round some bends we come to the last place where the River Frome is culverted under the canal right on the corner where the line turns away from the river valley and heads directly into

39. The same view looking east; from left to right the Daneway Inn, Bridge and the wharfhouse. A timeless view capturing much of the character of the Thames & Severn in its later years. Date c. 1904.

the hillside and Sapperton tunnel. On the right just before the entrance is a lengthsman's cottage, now alas seriously vandalised; the building is unsafe and must have a doubtful future, although it would be a pity to lose this link with the history of the tunnel. The cottage was lived in until the early 1970s despite the absence of any main services. From the side of the cottage, a track leads to the Daneway-Sapperton road and provides a point of access to this section. Another footpath strikes obliquely up the hillside to the left to Sapperton village which is well worth a visit.

Sapperton Tunnel is certainly the most impressive achievement in the construction of the Thames & Severn and also the most difficult and expensive. The story of its building in 1784-9 is intimately tied up with both success and failure. At first the Canal Company made the error of contracting with one Charles Jones to undertake the work; although well recommended, Jones proved to be over-ambitious and incapable of the major task of driving a tunnel over two miles long. After bitter wrangles, the proprietors replaced him with others, and the records show that the small group of contractors, among them John Nock and Ralph Shepperd (who had constructed so much else of the line) finished the job. This is one reason why it all took so long, but it is quite easy today to

40. Approaching Sapperton tunnel with the village on the skyline c. 1904. Probably taken the same day as No. 39 by the Oxford photographer H.W. Taunt.

146

underestimate the scale of the achievement. In the later eighteenth century, tunnelling on this scale was still a rarity and Sapperton has still only been overtaken in length of tunnelling by two other canal tunnels and ten tunnels of the later (and perhaps more advanced) railway age. The actual depth below the surface is 200' in places, and the agreed length 3,817 yards. In surveying the original line, Robert Whitworth confessed that the tunnel would be 'an uncertain piece of business in point of expense' because of the nature of the rock, and his estimate of £36,575 was considerably exceeded.

It will immediately be obvious that there was no towpath through the tunnel and this was not in fact a feature generally found on canals until later. The method of working boats through has become part of the canal legend. They were 'legged' by men lying on the roof or prow of the boat and walking against the tunnel side or springing off the roof arch. On the broader Thames barges, this was easier to achieve than on the narrower boats in common use in later years, when a plank was extended on which the legger lay. Whilst all this was in progress the horses – or more usually donkeys – followed the footpaths over the

41. Daneway entrance to Sapperton tunnel c. 1902 with the tunnel cottages on the right. A popular postcard view for many years.

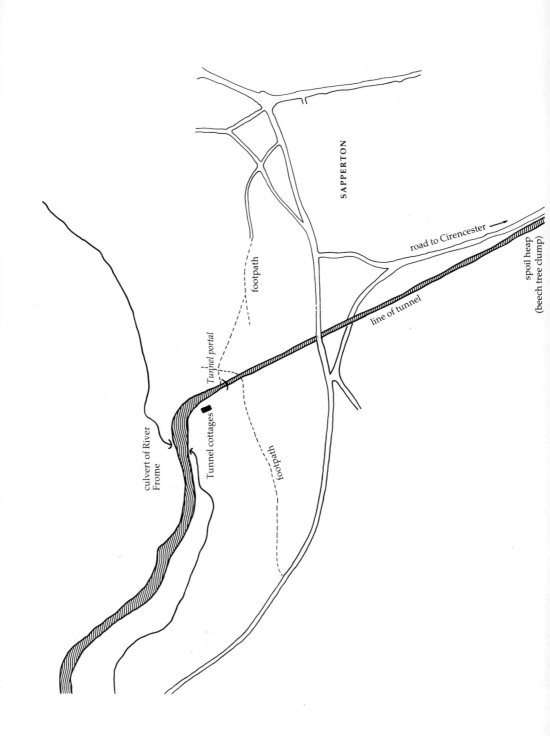

SAPPERTON

road to Cirencester

footpath

line of tunnel

spoil heap
(beech tree clump)

culvert of River
Frome

Tunnel portal

Tunnel cottages

footpath

summit from one tunnel entrance to the other. These paths are still known today as 'the donkey path' and our route will follow them in part.

Today the tunnel is blocked, most particularly in two places where large falls of rock (believed to be in 1916) effectively severed the through route. *It cannot be emphasised too strongly that access into the tunnel is not allowed and it remains private property and is in a dangerous condition.* The geology of the Cotswold hills at this point goes a long way in explaining some of the problems of maintenance in the tunnel. From this western or Sapperton entrance, a section runs through the notoriously unstable fuller's earth which had to be lined with brick and stone; a further section cut through the inferior oolite and remained unlined and spectacularly rock-cut. In the next long section through fuller's earth lining was again required and this became known as the Long Arching. To compound the problem, the lines of geological fault between these beds were themselves points of weakness. Restoration of the tunnel will form a major challenge to the Canal Trust in due course. The engineering feasibility study commissioned a few years ago accepted that this could be done with modern methods, although costs will no doubt prove to be considerable.

The area around the western entrance is one of the more recent work sites for Trust members, with the support of the Bathurst Estate as landowners. The canal bed is being cleaned up and some of the masonry walls rebuilt. It is hoped to begin work on the restoration of the tunnel portal using the professional skills of a local stone mason. The design of the portal is certainly interesting, and despite the vandalism, it is possible to appreciate the original design. This entrance was gothic in its detailing, presenting a sombre image to the canal traveller. The top was battlemented and the many old photographs of this area show this quite well. Imagine the sense of awe with which a nineteenth century boatman entered the tunnel through this battlemented arch! Hard by the entrance is the milestone WALBRIDGE 7½ INGLESHAM 21¼ – the plate a victim of theft in the last few years.

Sapperton to Coates (above the tunnel)

Leaving the tunnel, take the footpath to the right up to the road, turning left here up the hill to the crossroads at the edge of Sapperton village. A walk through the village and visit to the church can be recommended, but our route takes us towards Cirencester. After about a quarter of a mile the entrance to Manor Farm on the left is a pointer to the first of the line of spoil heaps just over in the fields on the right. These mark the position of vertical shafts dug down to the canal level and used as fixed points from which the horizontal cutting was carried out. In deference to the wishes (implied if not expressed) of the landowner Lord Bathurst,

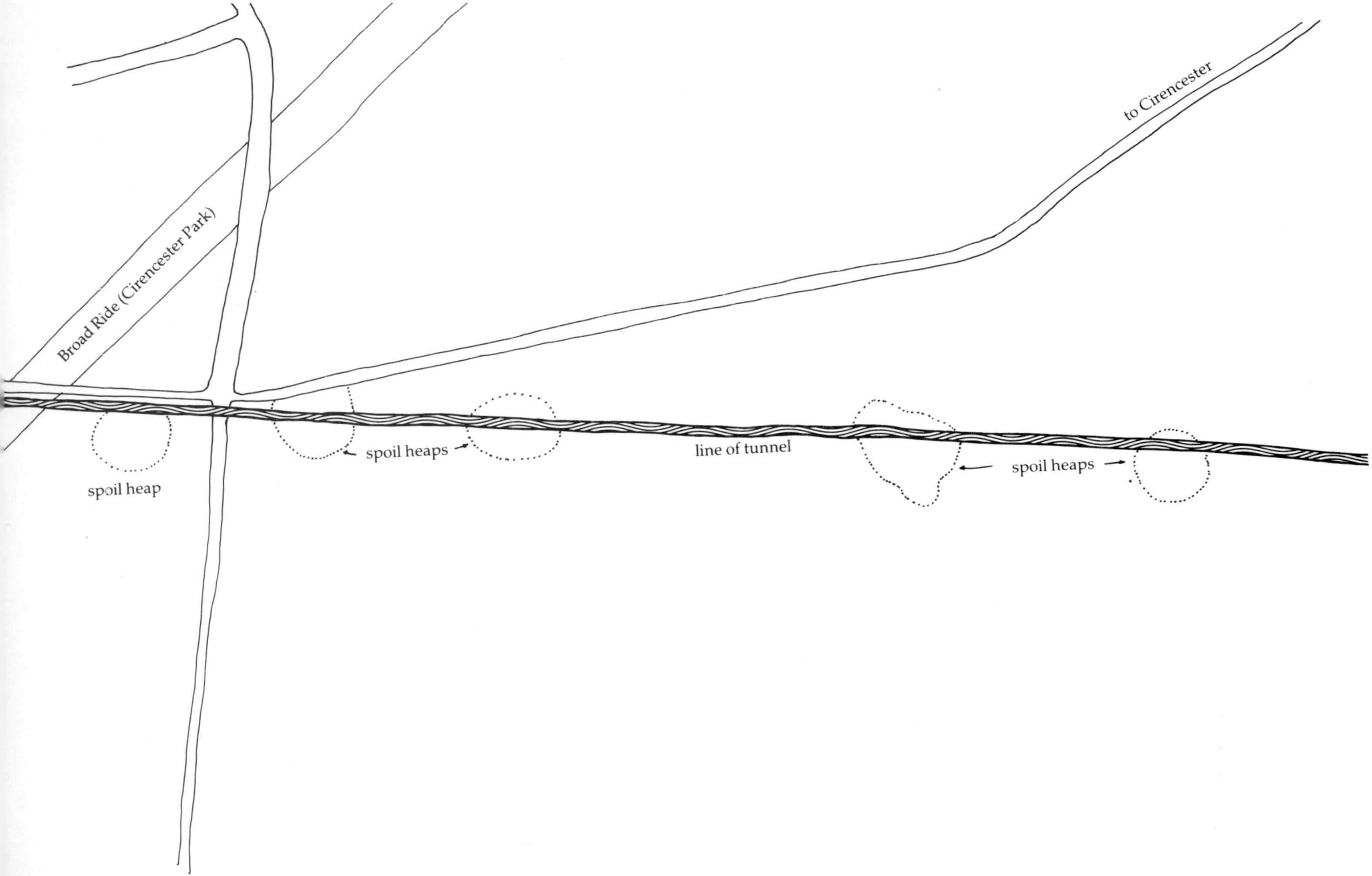

spoil heap

Broad Ride (Cirencester Park)

spoil heaps

spoil heaps

line of tunnel

spoil heaps

spoil heaps

to Cirencester

the canal proprietors arranged for these spoil heaps to be planted with beech trees and they now form a distinct feature of the local landscape.

It will be obvious that no right of way exists along the actual line of the shafts and spoil tips. However, the alignment can best be appreciated from the road as we leave the village. Incidentally, note the crossing of the line of Broad Ride, a straight tree-lined avenue in Cirencester Park extending some five miles from Sapperton common here all the way to Cirencester. This is itself a superb walk on another occasion. Keep an eye across to the right as the road bends gently left, where the view across the valley takes in the canal line very well indeed. One fixed point is the modern bungalow in the bottom; this is Tumbledown (rebuilt now!) beyond which a scrub-covered mound in the field marks one of the shafts. The bungalow actually stands virtually on the line of the tunnel. Some of the spoil heaps here reveal the grey material of the fuller's earth beds below; once again, we must say that these heaps remain dangerous. Although all the shafts were originally filled in, some were reopened at the end of the last century for repair work and all require great caution in exploration. We would recommend leaving them well alone.

From the junction with the main Stroud-Cirencester road, cross over and proceed a little way to the left. Opposite the lodge, a number of routes enter Hailey Wood, part of Cirencester Park, and accessible to walkers. Reference to the OS map is recommended in order to negotiate the woods successfully to the Tunnel House, but a general line followed south-westerly ought to bring the walker to the bridge across the railway at 163 : SO 962013, when a left turn immediately after the bridge should be taken.

Four pathways converge at this point and immediately opposite and safely within a wire fence is an open tunnel shaft; perhaps this was left open for ventilation purposes and has been lined by stone walling. (It remains a dangerous structure). It is also at this point that the canal tunnel crosses under the railway line. Follow the path alongside the railway line which is dropping steadily down towards Kemble. The deep cutting at one point exposes interesting geological layers. On the right spoil tips, sometimes bare of trees, can be made out before we pass a railway bridge and join the track for the final stretch to Tunnel House.

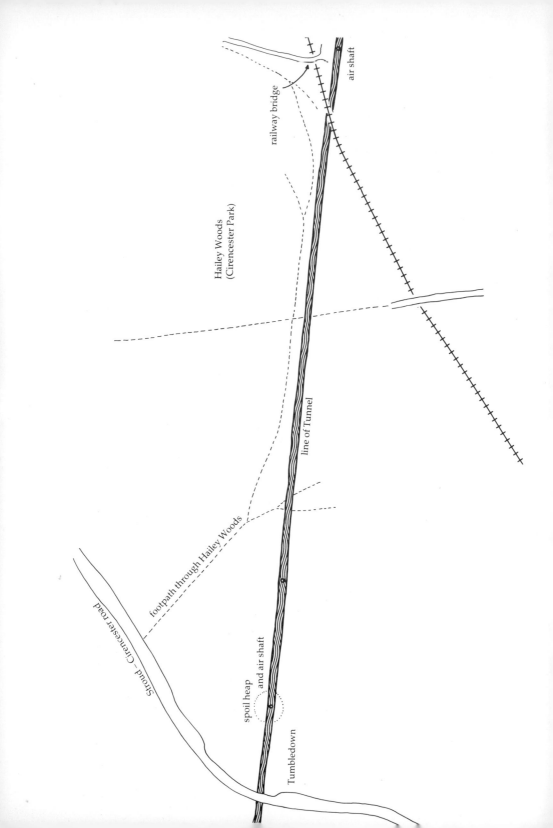

CHAPTER TWELVE

Coates to Smerrill

Coates portal of the tunnel is now most impressive. Probably it was always intended to be so, to act as something of a showpiece for the Thames & Severn. The detailing is classical in style; indeed it seems to represent a sort of check-list of classical features one might expect to see: a central pediment with flanking classical columns and finials, two niches, plus two circular and a central rectangular entablature. All this seems to sit atop the actual tunnel mouth set well down into the cut. It is very striking, and particularly so since the Trust made the bold and enterprising decision to raise funds for the restoration of the portal in 1976-7. The full story has been told elsewhere (see Further Reading) but at a cost of something over £6,000 local mason Bruce Russell with the aid of a job creation team undertook the recovery of much of the masonry from the canal bed, its repair and re-use. A relatively small amount of new stone was used, and already this is blending in with the original. The formal unveiling by Lord Bathurst in July 1977 must be regarded as one of the highlights of restoration so far, and the tidying up of this stretch and activities along the next section give some indication of the potential improvements which restoration can bring. A small metal grille now seals off the tunnel entrance to prevent access. Information on Trust activities can usually be obtained during summer weekends from the sales caravan sited near the portal. A range of publications is also available.

Immediately above the portal is the Tunnel House Inn. As with Daneway, this too was built during the construction period of the canal to house workers. It was then called the New Inn and also provided stabling for horses behind the inn – all now cleared away. Perhaps the greatest tragedy was a severe fire in 1952 which gutted the building. Reconstruction of the inn as we now see it excludes the old third floor – the lodging accommodation – but Tunnel House still retains something of an isolated atmosphere between woods and the open Cotswold countryside.

> Access: this is best made from the rough gravelled track signposted from the road between Coates and Tarlton villages just beyond the sharp bend in the road beneath the railway line.

Looking down the canal from the portal the cutting stretches away in a straight line to Tarlton Bridge and is known as the Kings Reach following a visit here by King George III in 1788 when he 'expressed the most decided astonishment and commendation' at the work in progress. The towpath restarts on the right hand side and will now stay on this side all the rest of the way to Inglesham. It is only in the cutting that the grandeur of the canal works here can be fully appreciated, with bare rock exposed on the bankside. Close to the tunnel entrance is a barge layby for boats to tie up and await their turn to navigate the tunnel. Through passage was by four hourly periods each way throughout the day and night and was slightly quicker from east to west with the flow of water from the main feeders for the summit level on this side of the tunnel, primarily of course from the Thames Head pumping station. An umbrella of beech trees sheltered the cutting for many years but clearance of dead trees and routine forestry management opened up the area during 1976. The imagination should be allowed to run away a little here to visualise the sheer hard work the canal navvies put in to build this section with only hand tools – picks, shovels and wheelbarrows.

42. Tunnel House Inn at Coates in April 1947 a few years before the fire which badly damaged the building.

It should also be noted that the whole canal bed is lined with concrete. This was a major area of activity during the County Council period of restoration from 1902 onwards in the battle against water leakage through fissures in the rock. The concrete lining here was a complete success (it still is) and the Council even considered such lining for the whole canal in order to rid themselves of their greatest problem. However, the estimate of nearly £73,000 caused consternation and the idea was soon dropped. Seventy-five years later, we might contemplate that this was the real turning point, when the last authority to struggle with the canal's water problems finally gave up and backed out.

This concreted section down to Tarlton Bridge was cleared out and repaired by the Trust in 1975-7 hence the sloping ramp into the canal bed to give access for equipment etc. This ramp is to be left in position as a slipway for the launching of boats into this section, which has already been 'christened' with at least one small craft. Beneath Tarlton Bridge the insertion of stop planks holds back a good depth of water flowing from the tunnel. The bridge has always been kept in good condition as a

43. Coates entrance to Sapperton tunnel c. 1904 and photographed possibly on the same day as Nos. 39 and 40.

155

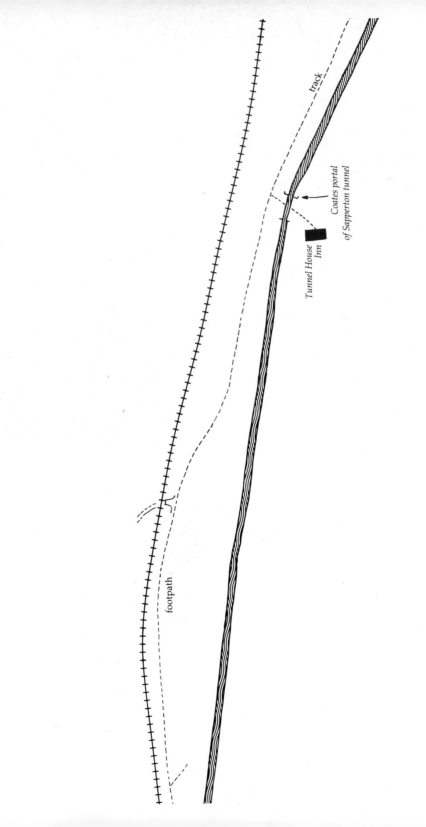

track

Coates portal
of Sapperton tunnel

Tunnel House
Inn

footpath

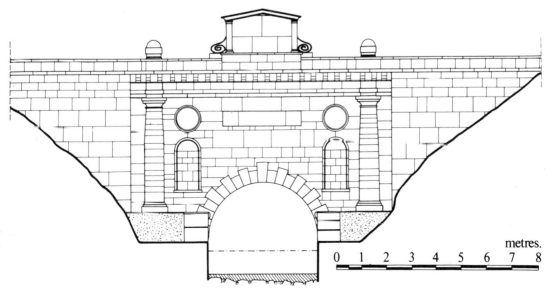

44. Restoration . . . work in progress on the Coates portal of Sapperton
tunnel in 1976/7 by the Stroudwater, Thames & Severn Canal Trust. The
portal has now been fully restored to its original condition.

metres.

0 1 2 3 4 5 6 7 8

158

45. *Woodland setting for the Kings Reach at Coates with the boat layby in the foreground. Looking away from the tunnel entrance.*

road bridge and is a point of access to the towpath. From here it is possible to appreciate something of the style of this bridge rebuilt in 1823 and an excellent foil to the portal beyond. The canal now swings round to a west/east alignment into a deep cutting; the towpath, however, rises up following the lie of the land here. There are a number of bad examples of rock fissures in the canal bed, currently under investigation by the Trust. These could often act as 'blow holes' bursting the clay lining of the bed by water pressure. This section also includes a prominent milestone, again minus its plate, but recording the tenth mile from Wallbridge.

A programme of clay re-puddling was carried out along here in 1902-4, and recent Trust activity has included clearance of the bed and attention to the position of the stop-gate by the roundhouse. The insertion of a small dam here marks the end of active work on the summit level for the time being. Single stop-gates were provided at five points along the summit level from the outset for the obvious purpose of controlling water flow in this all-important reservoir and in limiting losses when leaks broke out. The original intention was that a self-acting gate would close off a section when a sudden flow of water occurred. In practice this was not guaranteed (a maintenance problem, again?) and they were replaced by the simple plank-stop, a waisted masonry abutment with a vertical groove for the insertion of a row of planks, stored nearby. Ultimately there were eighteen of these along the summit and they can be spotted at strategic points.

Coates roundhouse is a very interesting comparison with the first example we have seen at Chalford. It has the same dimensions and internal layout, but the roof arrangement is different. Instead of the upright conical shape, the roof here (and incidentally at two other roundhouses) was inverted, the whole arrangement concealed behind the circular wall of the building. In such an isolated spot as Coates, this was of course the most successful way of gathering a water supply, piped off the roof into water storage at ground level. Although this building is now derelict (and dangerous) the internal layout was recorded some years ago before the roof pattern finally disintegrated. Again, the ground floor began life as a stable with living accommodation above. A scullery addition at the rear in later years indicates a change of use and a greater amount of room for domestic accommodation. Of all the interesting buildings along the line of the Thames & Severn, this little structure most demands maintenance to prevent further deterioration; can nothing be done?

Just beyond, the canal and towpath passes under a lofty-arched railway bridge, particularly notable for its skew-bridge arrangement, built by the railway engineers when the Swindon to Cheltenham line was pushed through to Stroud and Gloucester in the early 1840s. Well

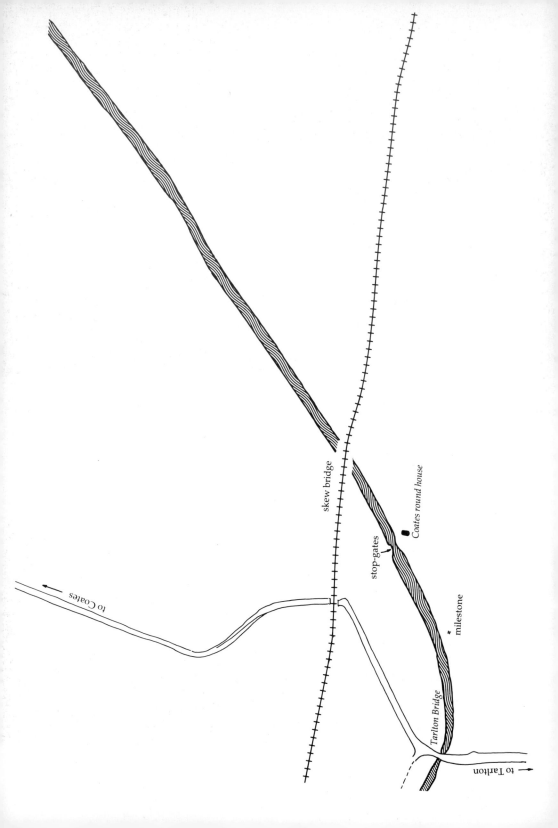

skew bridge

stop-gates

Coates round house

milestone

to Coates

Tarlton Bridge

to Tarlton

*46. Tarlton Road bridge at the end of the Kings Reach section. Rebuilt in
1823 this bridge survives as an excellent canal feature.*

*47. Coates roundhouse on the summit level with the G.W.R. line crossing
behind. The date is 1938.*

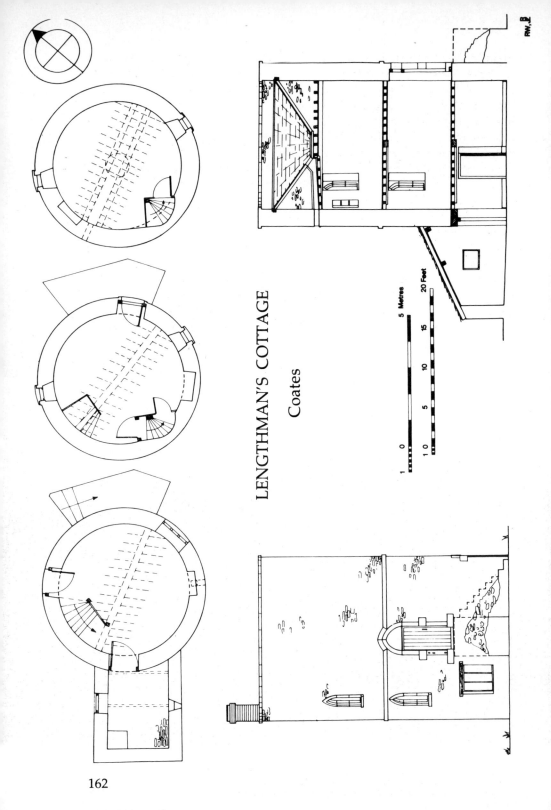

LENGTHMAN'S COTTAGE

Coates

RW.B

5 Metres

20 Feet

162

maintained by British Rail (out of necessity) it repays study as a remarkable brick construction. The canal summit level is now following the 365′ contour line and turns into the very upper reaches of the Thames Valley. A straight stretch for half a mile leads towards Trewsbury Bridge and although this section is fairly easy to see the towpath has become much less easy to walk despite being a right of way. The canal bed remains very dry even in wet weather and this serves to illustrate how bad this section was for water retention. This very stretch was the cause of Robert Whitworth's reference to 'bad rocky ground' when carrying out the original survey.

At the bridge we reach the furthest point east of the continuous run of right of way (the tunnel apart) which we have enjoyed all the way from Stroud. From here on the towpath cannot be guaranteed to be a right of way and there will be many examples of the loss of access resulting from the sale of the canal to landowners on either side of the line. Often this division was achieved actually down the centre of the canal bed and in these circumstances we must not be surprised that reclamation for agricultural use has involved the elimination of the towpath. However, more of this later on . . .

48. Another of the 1896 group of survey photographs, illustrating Whitworth's section of 'bad, rocky ground' on the summit level in Coates Field east of the roundhouse. The G.W.R. skew bridge prominent in the background.

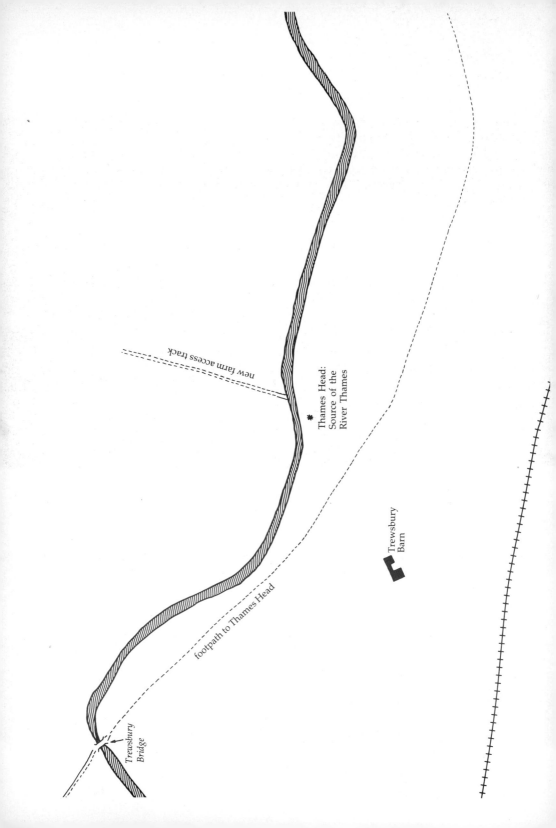

new farm access track

Thames Head:
Source of the
River Thames

Trewsbury
Barn

footpath to Thames Head

Trewsbury
Bridge

Access: this section can be reached by a footpath signposted from the road into Coates from the A433 Cirencester-Tetbury road. It is part of the route to Thames Head which we will be following shortly.

The sharp turn to the right immediately after Trewsbury bridge has left its mark on the rubbing stones beneath the bridge arch; here the tow-ropes were strained against the bridge as the horse-drawn barges negotiated the bend. From here on the towpath is effectively impassable and the route should now follow the footpath off the bridge into the fields to the right. This actually follows the canal line but at a slightly lower level until it reaches the celebrated source of the river at Thames Head. There is not enough space here to argue the pros and cons of the actual source of this famous river, but this remains the official source, and was marked until recently by the reclining figure of Old Father Thames. Despite his scowls, youthful vandalism played its all too familiar role and the Thames Commissioners opted for a safer resting place for this source of inspiration (if not always of water) at St. John's

49. *Thames Head Bridge where the Cirencester–Tetbury road crosses the canal. Wharf buildings on the right. The bridge survives with the canal culverted under the re-aligned road.*

165

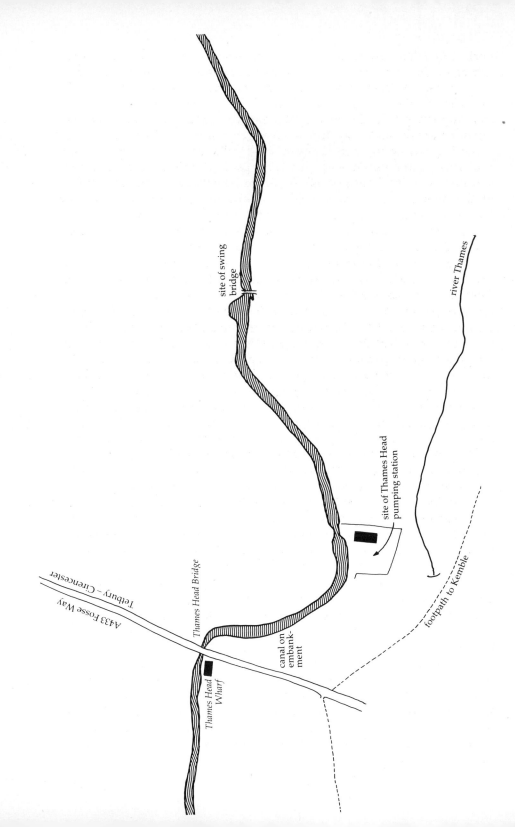

site of swing
bridge

river Thames

site of Thames Head
pumping station

Thames Head Bridge

A433 Fosse Way
Tetbury – Cirencester

footpath to Kemble

canal on
embank-
ment

Thames Head
Wharf

Lock at Lechlade. In his place an explanatory plaque stands beneath an ash tree. Doubtless this is a big disappointment to many summer visitors but the time to appreciate the niceties of the discussion is in mid-winter when the whole of the valley floor in which we are now standing is regularly flooded right across the pasture fields. Up on the left a breach through the canal bank for farm access to Trewsbury also allows a glimpse of the cottage built in the old quarry here, part of the bed of the canal now being used for a garden. This area is obviously private but notice that the cut through the canal bank reveals something of the stratigraphy of construction – the grey clay puddle and the foundations on which the towpath and boundary wall were built.

The footpath route across these meadows follows the valley floor, whilst the canal remains with the contour line higher up on the left. Before long the A433 road is reached, which is here following the line of the 2,000 year old Fosse Way south-westwards from the Roman town of Cirencester. On the left as we approach the road, notice the buildings of the Thames Head wharf and the embankment upon which the road crosses the river valley. It might also be possible to spot the small culvert through which the infant river is piped beneath the road. Turn left up to the wharf, taking great care along this fast and busy stretch of the main road. There are several interesting details to study at the wharf buildings, which are private property. The house is not readily associated with the canal except by its position, and indeed this wharf serves no immediate area but was intended rather to provide access to the main road and thence to Tetbury and beyond. The wharfhouse was probably built by the mason John Holland in 1784 for the resident agent, a post which only survived until about 1835 when the amount of trade could no longer justify its retention. There was also a small warehouse and some stables. Also, note the survival of the original canal bridge here and a section of the old road over it. County Council road improvements in 1962 thoughtfully included bridge preservation and a plaque records the fact. Although the bridge hole seems largely buried, the canal bed is now piped beneath the road.

Another sharp turn in the line of the canal takes place immediately after the road crossing, whence the line is contoured around the hillside to the site of the pumping station at Thames Head. Both the driveway along the canal bed and indeed the pump house now form *a private residence and there is no public access along this section.* In fact, the arrangements as they survive can just as well be appreciated by returning down the slope to the stone stile from the main road signposted to Kemble. We are again following through the fields along the line of the river, and a fine old parish boundary stone can be discovered preserved in the bank below the road near where the culvert re-appears; this marked the ancient boundary between Coates and Kemble.

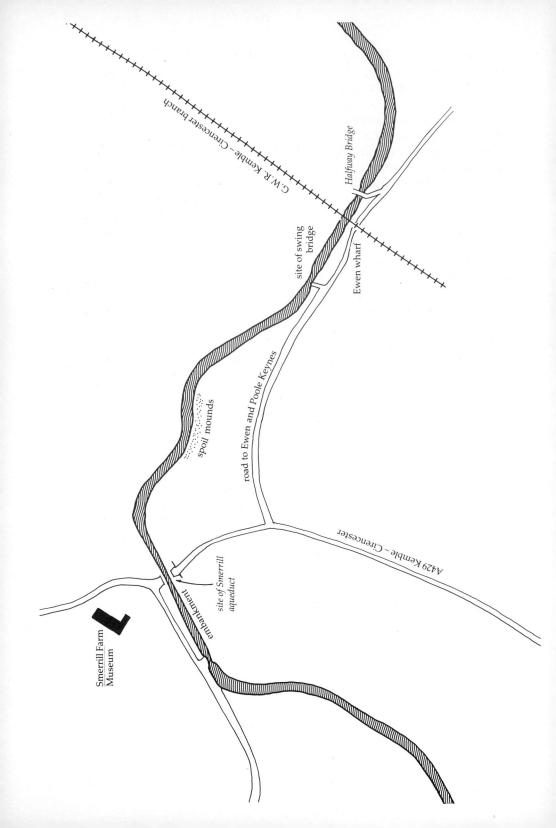

As the canal, now high up on the embankment to the left, turns due east the enlarged and virtually rebuilt Pump House comes into view; this as recently as 1974 changed completely the character of Thames Head, where the engineman's house had been virtually the only surviving building of interest. Very little now remains to tell the story of the successive pumping arrangements here, as the last engine and boiler houses have been demolished and the open well filled in. The need for pumping into the summit level was obvious to the Canal Company from its early days, the intended supply into the summit from the river Churn at Cirencester being too spasmodic and fraught with difficulties. In 1791, only two years after opening the canal, the Company installed a Boulton and Watt beam engine and pump. This was later replaced by a more efficient second-hand Cornish engine and pump in 1854. Both engines pumped water from a large oval well 64' deep dug into the floor of the valley. There were eventually many underground culverts linked back to this well to maintain a supply. The well never ran dry even when pumped continually in the dry summer months, when up to three million gallons of water could be taken up into the canal per day. The last engine and pump worked up until 1912 by which time navigation in the summit level was finished and the engine and pump were finally scrapped in 1941 in the scrap metal drive during the war.

From here the canal continues to follow the contour winding away to the left to the head of a small side valley which it was able to cross at Smerrill with the minimum of embankment construction. The footpath however remains firmly with the line of the river and passes a wind-pump at Lyd Well – itself a significant source of water to this area. The bed of the river has deepened steadily and is influenced by the outflow from the four main springs of water; eventually the A429 Cirencester-Kemble road is reached, where the river goes beneath the road via a fine piece of culverting (put in when the railway was built in 1841). We can now only imagine the arrangement here when the railway was carried high over both river and road with the branch line into Cirencester.

Access: this is easily found on the A429, and represents the best point at which to forsake walking in favour of a car for the next sections of canal. Only limited bus services use this road but Kemble station (British Rail) is within easy walking distance. Trains from here to Swindon, Gloucester and beyond – the station buildings are themselves worth a visit.

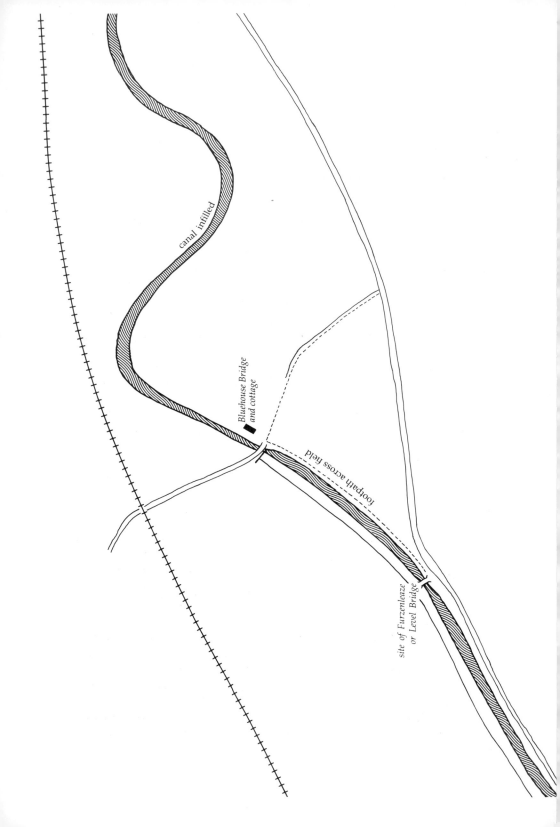

canal infilled

Bluehouse Bridge
and cottage

footpath across field

site of Furzenleaze
or Level Bridge

for the nearby house; perhaps a small wharf existed here to supply the village of Ewen along the road. From this point the line of the canal around to Park Leaze Bridge is both *private property* and very overgrown with nothing of interest to see. Instead follow by road almost into Ewen, then double back sharply left towards Siddington and Cirencester; this road soon comes to the canal again. When the road turns sharply to the right, a farm road straight ahead soon crosses the site of Park Leaze Bridge. Unfortunately this has been levelled – a pity as the bridge was quite an attractive feature here.

Along this section between Thames Head and Upper Siddington, there is only one bridge – at Halfway – surviving of the total of nine. In fact for the whole of the eastern section from Coates to Inglesham only sixteen of the forty-two bridge crossings remain intact, whereas the western line up to Sapperton from Stroud still has twenty of the thirty-one remaining. This fact alone illustrates very clearly the varying fortunes of the two sections of the Thames & Severn.

The road towards Cirencester runs alongside the canal for some distance and although overgrown it is possible to look down into the cutting where the canal bed usually holds water here. This must seep in from either side as this section is completely cut off at either end from the rest of the line. The end of this section is marked by the site of Furzenleaze or Level Bridge, so named because the canal was down in a cutting. From here, canal and road part company and one could be forgiven for doubting that the canal ever existed. Much of the next mile or so was filled in by Cirencester Urban and Rural District Councils using the length as a rubbish tip for a number of years. Only a slight dip in the fields and (best clue) the hedge lines remain to give any indication on the ground.

From further along the road, a footpath (unfortunately not sign-posted) follows the towpath line across a field to Bluehouse Bridge. Look left for the roof top of the cottage and the route becomes reasonably clear. An attempt to rationalise this right of way around the road was defeated recently and although short, this is another link preserved in the chain. Actually, the canal was in a cutting here and where filling took place it has sunk just enough to be detectable across the field. However there is absolutely no trace of the considerable activity here in 1902-4 when contractors dug out clay and repuddled sections of this length. The bridge has been levelled but the lengthman's cottage survives, now known as Copsefield and *private property*. Extensions in recent years are obvious but note particularly the way in which the building was originally constructed into the canal bank. Future restoration along this section might well take the form of cutting a new and shorter alignment.

Beyond Bluehouse, where the garden now occupies the canal bed,

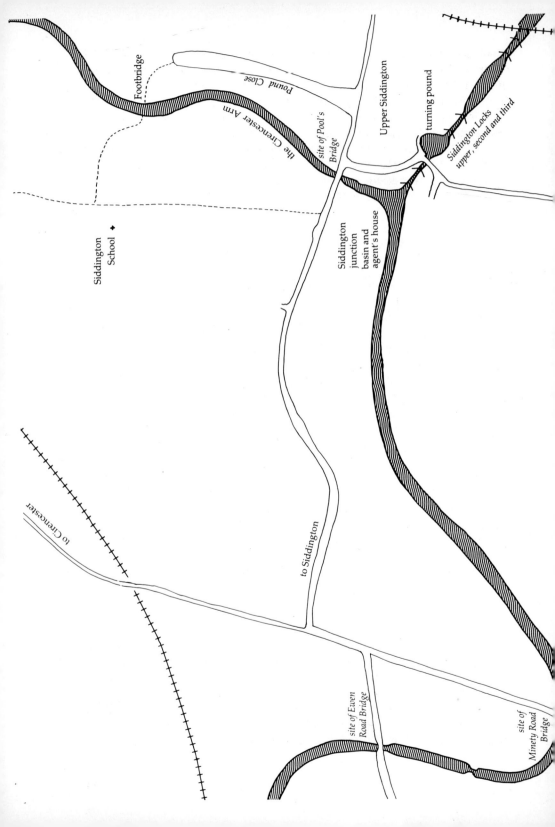

Footbridge

the Cirencester Arm

Pound Close

site of Pool's Bridge

Upper Siddington

turning pound

Siddington Locks
upper, second and third

Siddington School

Siddington junction basin and agent's house

to Siddington

to Cirencester

site of Ewen Road Bridge

site of Minety Road Bridge

there is nothing of note in the infilled section which follows two large S-bends along the contours here. The line is picked up again at the site of Ewen Road Bridge and across one more field to Minety Road Bridge. Both have now been levelled and indeed were points of access to the town refuse tip along this section. From the road junction between the two canal crossing points of the road, turn left and then immediately right towards Siddington. En-route to the village the canal line can be seen over to the right marked by a line of trees. At Upper Siddington, turn right by the playing fields (crossing incidentally the Cirencester canal arm, of which more below) to join the canal at the Siddington flight of locks.

Access: Siddington is just south of Cirencester and a good point of access by car for exploration of the eastern section. Limited parking above the playing fields.

From the bridge at the tail of Siddington Upper Lock, it is possible to appreciate the layout. Note firstly the good state of preservation of this brick bridge, including a rather attractive small detail; the iron clamps holding the coping stones on the bridge parapet are stamped TSC, initials which can also be found on bricks, boundary stones etc. elsewhere. Immediately above the lock, and not easily accessible, is the junction basin of the main line of the canal with the short arm off to the right into Cirencester. Both lock chamber and basin have recently been cleaned out. On the right and facing the basin is the former agent's house, an important canal building because here lived the Company's agent. The workshop for the canal's eastern section was also here. Meticulous records kept here at the very eastern end of the summit level give a fascinating picture of the trade passing east and west along the canal and indeed also on the Cirencester arm. Not the least useful were the reports back to Brimscombe of the depth of water on the sill of the top lock here; this gave some idea of the levels in the summit and intending travellers could plan accordingly. These records are preserved along with all the other Canal Company records in the Gloucestershire Record Office and form one of the best collections of records for any canal in Britain.

The Cirencester Arm

Although a branch from the main line, this is an appropriate point to explore the one and a quarter mile Cirencester section, working north from Siddington junction. There are two major factors governing our study of this short but important arm. The first is that the considerable growth of Cirencester in the past two decades has removed most if not all of the evidence of the canal in the town. The second point is that the arm was part of the summit level, and indeed an important part of it.

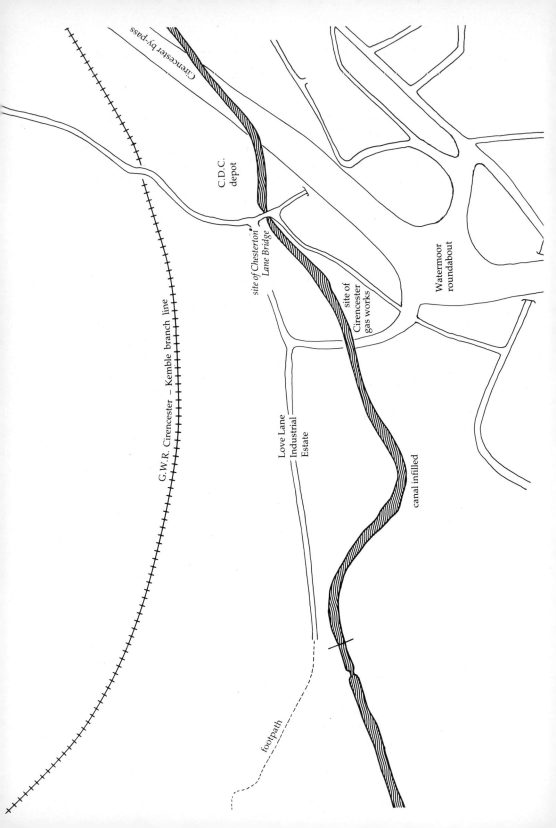

G.W.R. Cirencester – Kemble branch line

(Cirencester by-pass)

C.D.C. depot

site of Chesterton Lane Bridge

site of Cirencester gas works

Watermoor roundabout

Love Lane Industrial Estate

canal infilled

footpath

Apart from the obvious desire to link up with the trade prospects of this market town, the Cirencester link was also built to gain access to the waters of the river Churn and thus to ensure (it was hoped) a good supply of water into the summit level.

In the 1950s and 60s, Cirencester adopted an area around Love Lane to the south of the town as the site for its industrial estate and this has now developed considerably. Unfortunately, the line of the canal ran right through this area, so that much has now been obliterated. However, a short stretch from Siddington is certainly worth exploring. Between the Canal House and the Ewen road a cottage and a modern house obscure the canal line and the road crossing marks the site of Pools Bridge, long since levelled. Opposite the infilled line can just be made out skirting a field running north. As this is now something of a local dump it is probably better to deviate slightly to the right into the housing estate at Pound Close. Follow this through to the far end where a footpath to Siddington school actually crosses the canal line. The present footbridge here is now less interesting than its predecessor, the girder-bridge having been dropped into the canal bed some years ago. The next half-mile or so is the only section not infilled and holds water at certain times; perhaps this is something of a mixed blessing as the presence of the industrial estate is now all too evident. Considering the significance of Cirencester in the history of the Thames & Severn, it is a pity that this sole surviving open section of the arm is so neglected and misused.

At a plank-stop, the infilling begins and the path emerges into Love Lane by joining a footpath which has come across the fields from the school. Once over the stile, the road should be followed straight ahead towards the town. There is no point in deviating here; keep straight ahead as the modern road comes in from the right at Cirencester Garage and continue until the Cotswold District Council depot (an old NAAFI incidentally) comes into sight. At this point, where the road swings round to the left, stood Chesterton Lane Bridge. The old line of this road is now truncated off to the right, although it is worth turning hard right to see the 'round house' close to the entrance to the GCC highways depot in Bridge Road. This interesting little building has often been assumed locally to be connected with the canal, probably because of the association with the other roundhouses. In fact it is not that shape but merely round-fronted because it was built in a sharp junction between the line of the canal (on its right) and Bridge Road or Gas Lane on its left. This latter is the clue as it was the Gas House and part of Cirencester Gas Works on this site. The cottage survives, but the distribution of gas is no longer a local responsibility.

Returning towards Cirencester, look for a flight of steps down to the right of the CDC depot which returns us to the towpath once again.

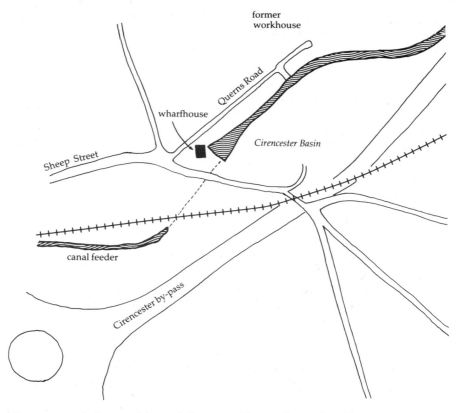

These record the position of the steps down from the Chesterton Lane Bridge at this point. An all too brief section of towpath follows (rather fenced in) before it is time to negotiate the Cirencester ring road cutting obliquely across the canal line. The underpass should be used but remember to keep the canal line firmly in mind when emerging the other side, for a housing development of recent years now encloses the old line. Actually the towpath route survives through this area almost intact and it is a pity that its original function is not recorded in some way, by name or perhaps plaque. En route, one short section of the boundary wall survives in Rutland Place.

Crossing into Querns Road, the canal line ran behind the gardens on the left, but new building here is finally obscuring the evidence. The site of Cirencester Wharf is even less interesting now. A modern building and yard cover the triangular site in the junction of Querns Road/ Querns Lane/Querns Hill, the building standing more or less on the site of the wharfinger house. This was a terminal basin at the head of arm, and boasted quite a range of buildings, plus a wooden crane. Some record was made before the largely derelict wharf house was demolished in 1975, and a measured drawing and photographs were included in the author's photographic album in that year (see Further Reading). The house itself was interesting, and its layout will be paralleled later on by surviving examples at Cricklade and at Kempsford.

The basin was lined with stone blocks and formed an impressive structure. Into it from the west side ran two culverts which linked in a series of open leats and culverts for over a mile to the access point with the river Churn at Jenour's Mill or Barton mill on the western side of Cirencester. The route passed under Cirencester Park and was culverted under the railway yard across the road from the wharf when the railway came to Cirencester in 1841. This source of water was much discussed and argued over. The Act of Parliament 23 Geo III Cap. 38 established the Canal Company's right to the waters of the Churn at Jenour's Mill and the first Earl Bathurst promised to sell the mill for this purpose. A change of plan by his successor in 1785 disrupted negotiations at a time when the Canal Company had begun building, relying on this source of water as the principal supply for the summit level. Thus committed, the Company's men attempted to make the connection, with the result that each party worked to thwart the other's efforts. It was not until 1791 that an agreement was reached.

This allowed the Company to have control over the sluice and take water freely when there was a sufficient level for all consumers further down the river. Otherwise compensation was payable on an hourly basis to each of the mills concerned. For the nine mills below Jenour's affected in this way, the hourly rate was 6s. 5½d., and the average compensation paid out during the period 1796-1835 was about £350 p.a. – a heavy outlay for the Company. Even as late as 1904, when only five mills were still in operation, the compensation rate was 3s. 6½d. per hour. Such was the difficulty of obtaining the canal's essential ingredient.

Little remains today although the culvert has been exposed in places and the final open section through the Phoenix Way development was only being filled in at the time of writing. Much more could be said of the Cirencester arm, but reference should be made to the study 'Cirencester and the Thames & Severn Canal' mentioned in the Further Reading section.

Access: in Cirencester, the wharf site will be found at the far (western) end of Querns Lane. From the town centre follow Cricklade Street to the traffic lights, turn right and then sharp left at the T-Junction. This area has changed a great deal in recent years and the topography is difficult to relate to former times. However, one small consolation is the naming of Whitworth Road on part of the wharf area in honour of the Canal's early engineer.

50. Destruction . . . the wharfhouse at Cirencester basin shortly before demolition in September 1975. Much altered and neglected, the building's basic function as a warehouse with central living accommodation can still be appreciated.

CHAPTER FOURTEEN

Siddington to Cerney Wick

From the bridge over Siddington Upper Lock the towpath follows down the right hand side of the canal through the closely-linked group of locks here. Siddington Second, Third and Lower Locks follow in quick succession, the group of four taking the canal down 39' from the summit into the long eastern section to the Thames. These are therefore deep locks and should be treated with respect; they are not fenced off and are hazardous. Although the lock gates have largely disappeared a feature to note is the circular pound above both the Second and Third locks to increase the amount of water available in this restricted space for working the flight. The towpath has been cleared by local groups with the aid of the Trust and we soon come to the brick piers of the former railway bridge carrying the Midland & South Western Junction railway line from Swindon to Cirencester. This was opened through Siddington in 1883 and closed completely in 1964. Just below, the site of the Lower Lock has now disappeared under a modern house (built actually on the lock) and coping stones from the lockside now adorn a rockery in the garden! The towpath is funnelled between separate housing plots and it is difficult to accept that such infilling could have happened so recently, when restoration of the canal was being planned. Constant vigilance will be needed if further inroads are to be avoided.

At the crossing of the road from Siddington village to Ashton Keynes stood Greyhound Bridge, now levelled but named after the nearby inn. This is another good place to pause for refreshments (snacks etc.) and indeed the Greyhound must have served a useful purpose for boatmen working down the Siddington flight of locks. From here almost to South Cerney the line of the towpath is virtually impassable and remains on *private farmland*. The towpath line is actually marked as a public footpath on Ordnance Survey maps, but until such time as the line can be opened up again for public use a return to the car is recommended as far as the lock-house at South Cerney.

The features of the closed section are relatively few. In parts the cut continues to hold water fairly well (from the gravel beds beneath) and some small lengths have been cleared at the owner's expense to encourage wildlife. Cowground Bridge remains in fair condition although its parapets have dropped into the canal. A milestone com-

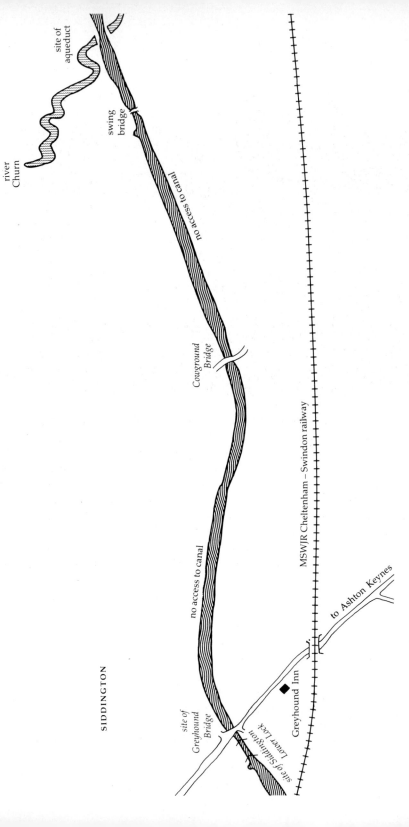

river
Churn

site of
aqueduct

swing
bridge

no access to canal

Cowground
Bridge

no access to canal

SIDDINGTON

MSWJR Cheltenham – Swindon railway

to Ashton Keynes

Greyhound Inn

site of
Greyhound
Bridge

site of Siddington
Lower Lock

plete with it plate WALBRIDGE 16 INGLESHAM 12¾ has been recovered from this section and was generously donated in 1971 by the landowner to the Corinium Museum in Cirencester for preservation. Other than the masonry abutments little remains of a swing bridge further along, and even less of the aqueduct carrying the canal across the river Churn. The river is here quite sizeable and the arch of the aqueduct was the cause of flooding during winter months from the backing up of water – hence its removal. In this section river and canal run close together, the latter on a slight embankment and clear of the problems of flooding. This area was locally known as 'the nooks' – a reference to the winding nature of the Churn.

A sharp turn on the line approaching our next point of contact took the canal through a deep cutting (largely overgrown) at Claymeadow, the name an indication of ground conditions here. The clay source was turned to advantage in a brick works established on the far side. Its products must at one time have been a feature of activities at South Cerney wharf where the cutting opens out and meets the Cirencester-South Cerney road. Incidentally, the line of the MSWJR has been running roughly parallel away to our right from Siddington on its route to Cricklade and Swindon.

It is possible to walk back from the road a little way to appreciate the

51. Between the locks at Siddington, looking to Upper Siddington and the junction with the Cirencester arm.

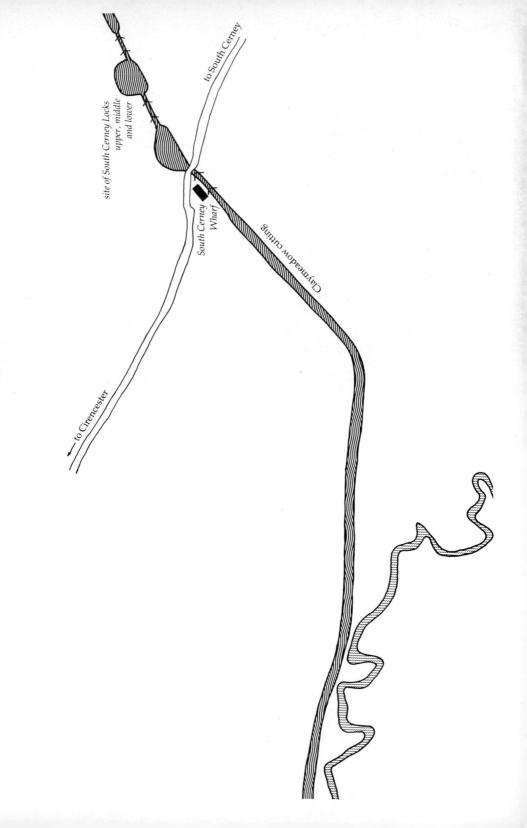

site of South Cerney Locks
upper, middle
and lower

to South Cerney

South Cerney
Wharf

Claymeadow cutting

to Cirencester

canal cutting and also gain a good view of the layout of the wharf, which
is now a *private house and garden*. The garden has been cleverly and
neatly created from the infilled Upper Lock, the top of three locks here.
The coping stones defining the lock sides of the chamber have been
retained. South Cerney enjoyed a lock-keeper who was also responsible
for the wharf and acted as lengthman. The wharf is actually some little
way out from the village but this was not unusual in the canal (and even
the railway) period. Its simple character is reminiscent of Thames Head
and the most interesting detail of the otherwise simple rectangular lock
cottage was a bay-window giving a good view over the lock. In the
modernisation of the property this feature has been developed still
further. From the wharfside, quantities of coal, timber, stone and
agricultural products (as well as the bricks) would have been trans-
ported away by farmer's cart and local wagon.

The bridge at the road crossing has completely disappeared and we
should now follow the footpath sign directing obliquely across the field
sloping gently away to the south east. En route it is possible to make out
from the irregular levels in the field the sites of South Cerney Middle

52. *At the bottom of the Siddington flight where the Midland & South
Western Junction Railway crossed. Very little sign of water in this 1896
view.*

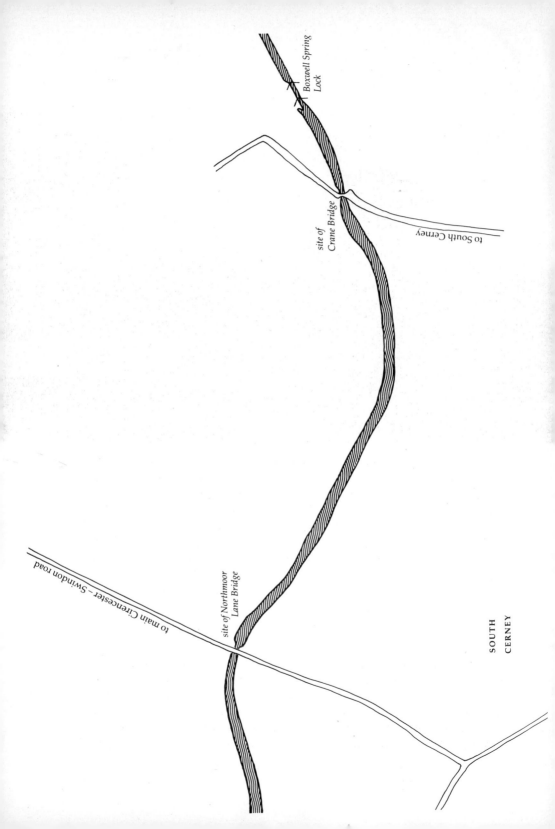

Boxwell Spring
Lock

site of
Crane Bridge

to South Cerney

site of Northmoor
Lane Bridge

to main Cirencester – Swindon road

SOUTH
CERNEY

and Lower Locks; each of the three had a fall of 9' 4". Although levelled and returned to agricultural use, these locks presumably remain reasonably intact beneath and might again be restored. Up to the left is South Cerney airfield, now in use by the Royal Corps of Transport, and one of the many airfields developed in this part of Gloucestershire in the years before the Second World War. We emerge onto the small lane linking the top of the village with the main A419 Cirencester-Swindon road. Northmoor Lane bridge here has also been levelled.

Access: this is a recommended starting point for an exploration on foot of the next section which can be walked right through to Latton basin, nearly four miles. Parking is restricted to the roadside and care should be taken.

At the road crossing the 'Public footpath' sign points towards one of the most attractive sections on the eastern part of the canal. The one-and-a-half miles to the Cotswold Water Park provides a leisurely and still relatively little-known walk of delightful seclusion, hidden from the nearby main road yet easy of access at either end. Almost immediately the path plunges into the undergrowth but the activities of

53. At the South Cerney group of locks . . . lock cottage and Upper Lock at the Wharf in the early years of this century.

187

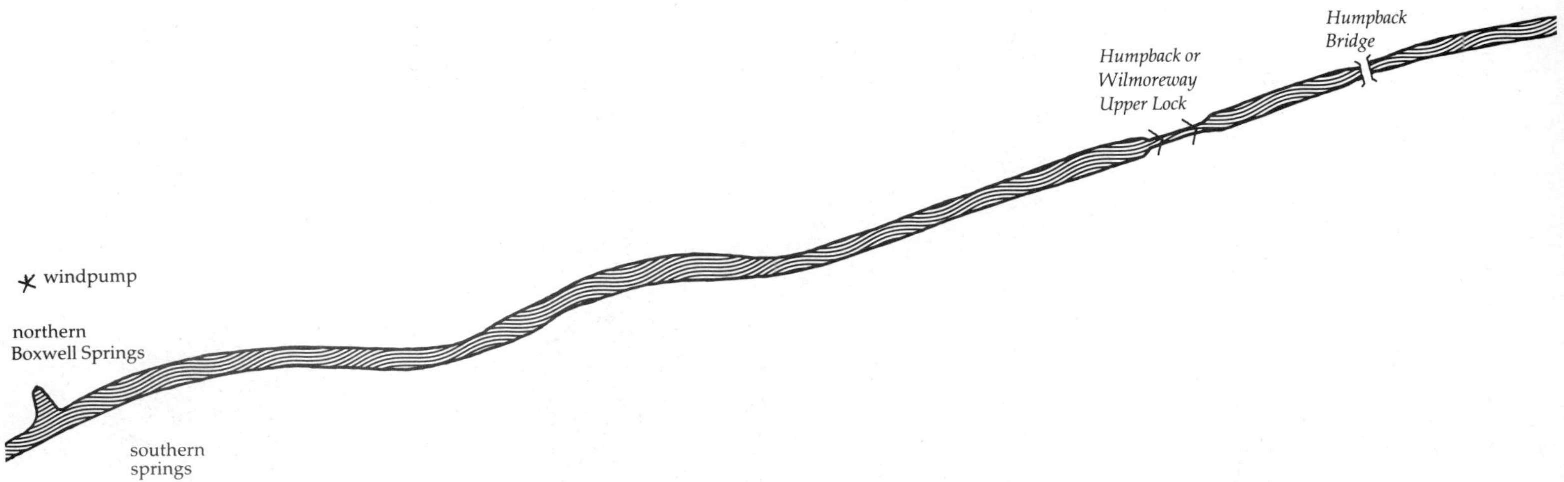

Humpback
Bridge

Humpback or
Wilmoreway
Upper Lock

✗ windpump

northern
Boxwell Springs

southern
springs

local amenity society members over the years have maintained access. The walk is in parts open with views to the level farmland on either side and at intervals shaded in 'groves' of tree growth which delight the eye particularly at high summer. There is however little by way of physical remains; at Crane Bridge, the road is now levelled; opposite the towpath runs along the access track to Crane Farm, an isolated building across the fields to the right. Along the track about half way to the farm gate, look in the hedge for the milestone WALBRIDGE 17½ INGLESHAM 11¼, one of the very few still retaining its original mileplate in situ – and long may it remain!

Shortly afterwards on the left is Boxwell Spring Lock, which makes its own particular contribution to the history of the Thames & Severn. Also known as Shallow or Little Lock, it has a fall of only 3' 6" which makes it – apart from the lower chamber at Dudgrove – the shallowest lock on the entire length. In fact Boxwell is an after-thought resulting from a miscalculation of the canal levels and water supplies here, and it was

54. . . . and further down, a rare sight of pleasure activity on the Thames & Severn c. 1875-85, passing into Lower Lock.

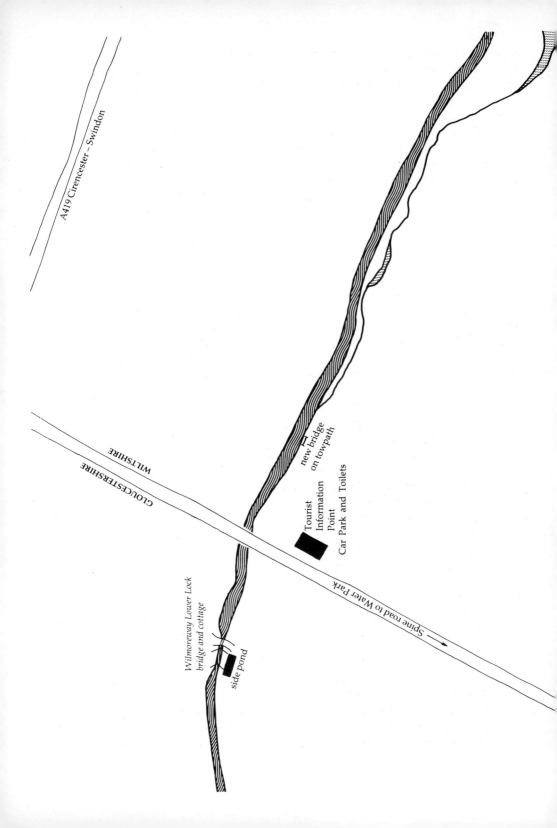

A419 Cirencester – Swindon

GLOUCESTERSHIRE

WILTSHIRE

new bridge
on towpath

Tourist
Information Point
Car Park and Toilets

Spine road to Water Park

Wilmoreway Lower Lock
bridge and cottage

side pond

inserted to lower the level of the canal bed in order to channel in water from the Boxwell springs nearby. Supplies were much needed along this stretch to meet the demands of the deep locks at Wilmoreway. Only one of the group of springs could thus be tapped, as the southern group, although more prolific, even with these alterations proved to be too far below the level of the canal. The new lock was built in 1792 by the mason Thomas Cook, for which he was paid (Household tells us) £86. 14s. 6d. It is interesting to note that Boxwell is a stone-lined lock in comparison with the heavy use of bricks elsewhere on this section. The pair of lower gates survive although in an advanced state of dereliction.

From the entrance to Crane Farm the towpath becomes a farm track and soon reverts to a footpath only. The site of the spring is in a small withy bed and in the field behind there is a derelict wind-pump which was obviously also sited onto these same water supplies. Off the towpath to the right are the more prolific southern springs. In the next length the restoration work of the Trust's eastern section working parties can be appreciated – the whole length from here through Wilmoreway to Cerney Wick and now to Latton basin has received attention during the last few years. Activity here has been restricted to clearance of the canal bed in some sections, towpath clearance all along the line, but has now turned to the more difficult tasks of lock repair, rebuilding and other structural problems. Just before Humpback or Wilmoreway Upper Lock an 'avenue' of trees lines the towpath in a most attractive manner. The lock has been cleared of debris and undergrowth and we can note the mixture of stone and brick in the chamber, testimony to many repairs. Also worth studying is the large overflow weir at the side of the towpath.

Below Humpback and past the collapsed red-brick Humpback Bridge the length is being checked for water retention by the Trust and includes some interesting experimental towpath restoration using a wattle principle. A splendid grove of ash trees brings us to Wilmoreway Lower Lock which had a fall of 11' producing a combined fall of 18' 6" for these last two locks which created considerable problems of water supply. One part of the solution to this problem can be seen to the right of the towpath down in the field alongside the lock. A large side pond was built here in 1831, and it is the only example on the eastern section of the canal. The pond was linked to the lock chamber by a large cast iron pipe so that by manipulation of the sluices about two-fifths of the water used in the lock could be drawn off for re-use. The pipe and cast iron lid can be seen clearly in the lock chamber, and in the corner of the side pond the other end which was until quite recently also covered by a cast iron lid. The side pond was lined with stone blocks but most have now disappeared. The other precaution taken to control water usage was the building of a lengthsman's cottage alongside the lock to ensure super-

careful eyes will see a milepost which would have shown us WAL-BRIDGE 19 INGLESHAM 9¾. It has a rounded head and carries a prominent benchmark carved onto it, but once again the mileage plate is missing. The group of white-painted buildings and tall white chimney over to the left are the Latton Creamery, once a flourishing milk processing plant, and a prominent feature in this flat landscape.

From here the canal bed has been colonised by a 'giant rhubarb', a plant thought to have 'escaped' from an Oxford botanical garden and over the years to have spread along rivers and canals; it now survives in such isolated locations. This dominates the canal bed for a considerable distance until a cleared section of canal indicates the approach to Cerney Wick. Recent clearance work here has included the felling of about forty diseased elm trees and has been followed by a general tidying up of the area.

55. *Roundhouse and lock at Cerney Wick before the restoration of the lock gates early this century.*

CHAPTER FIFTEEN

Cerney Wick to Marston Meysey

The roundhouse at Cerney Wick, the third example we have met along the canal so far, must be one of the canal's most attractive buildings and it certainly enlivens this less interesting section. It is remarkably well preserved and is obviously well looked after by its present owners. Its original layout can still be seen with a stable on the ground floor, a living room entered directly from steps on the first floor and bedrooms on the upper floor. The stone structure remains faced with stucco which together with the narrow gothic style windows and conical slate roof gives the building its now familiar characteristics. Even recent alterations have preserved the circular shape and a good touch is the stone ball-finial on top of the roof. The round-house, together with its garden alongside the lock and extending into the canal bed, is *private property and should be respected*. Indeed both the house and its setting can best be appreciated from the towpath side. The whole area is indeed a lucky survivor, for the lengthsman based here was moved up to Wilmoreway when that cottage was built in 1831 and the Cerney Wick roundhouse was no longer required. It passed out of canal ownership but in spite of that has stood the test of time rather better than its replacement.

Cerney Wick Lock with a fall of 6' has been the subject of recent Trust restoration activities with dredging and rebuilding. The rotting gates have been removed and the structure revealed as an interesting mixture of stone, red brick, and blue brick, indicating the various repairs carried out here over the years. The mason John Nock, whose men built so much of the canal, was paid £113 for building this lock and incidentally he built the next two locks down at Latton and Eisey. The bridge over the tail of the lock has been levelled. Close by, the Crown Inn is a good stopping place for refreshments along this section.

On the next stretch towards Latton the C.W.S. which owns this length has given permission for limited Trust restoration in order to clear the towpath and re-establish the right of way along it. This section is very isolated with no houses or roads in sight and probably the only interesting features are the two mileposts, one just below the lock and the other just before the basin at Latton. Certain parts of this section were never puddled with clay as the canal was cut through the

water-bearing gravel which lies just below the whole area here. At Latton Basin the large rectangular stone-lined basin is a surprise, sitting in a field on the other side of the River Churn. Its walls survive virtually intact except on the north side where the link with the canal by aqueduct across the river has been severed. The towpath bridge over this link has also disappeared. Now the river has an uninterrupted flow making the basin look like some gigantic error of judgement! The entrance to the North Wilts Canal just shows through the undergrowth at the far end and alongside stands the red brick toll cottage; its pantiled roof is in sharp contrast to the stone roofed cottages we have passed so far. This building is largely derelict and unsafe and much of the North Wilts Canal from this point is impassable.

The basin was formed in 1819 as part of a typical canal enterprise: the linking of two canal routes for the mutual benefit of both concerns. In fact the short length of the North Wilts Canal (nine miles) linked the Thames & Severn with the Wilts & Berks Canal at Swindon and thus gave an alternative and easier access to the Thames at Abingdon. The upper reaches of the Thames to Lechlade proved a problem for navigation throughout much of the life of the Thames & Severn, so much so that the proprietors were prepared to agree to, and pay for, the development at Latton even knowing that this link would cut out the

56. At Latton Basin — the junction with the North Wilts. Canal, entered through a pair of double stop-gates to control the water levels in each canal. Note the thatched ricks on the right.

remainder of their own canal between Latton and Lechlade. This new route was inextricably tied up with the fortunes of the Wilts & Berks Canal which by 1906 had incurred such losses that it was forced to close.

The lock from Latton Basin into the North Wilts is in fact not a true lock, but a pair of double stop-gates, one controlled by each company and indicative of the importance of water supply to each. The inevitable disputes arose about water levels, leading to argument and mis-use, when the gates would be held shut by one party against traffic from the other. From the track just to the east of the basin the onward line of the Thames & Severn Canal can be seen towards Cricklade from the levelled site of Weymoor Bridge.

> Access: to the basin can be made from the A419 Cirencester – Swindon road by following a track alongside Street Farm sign-posted to The Basin. Street Farm is virtually the last house on the Cirencester side of Latton, on the south side of the road.

The towpath walker should return to the main road, turn right and follow the path for about half a mile towards Court Farm. The roar of the traffic comes as a sharp reminder after the calm of the previous few miles! On the right, notice the former Latton mill and a little further on a milestone on the Cricklade – Cirencester turnpike at the entrance to the appropriately named Cotswold Gate. This reads CIRENr 6 CRICKe 1 and

57. A view of canal maintenance man 'Old Willum' working near Latton Basin in 1911.

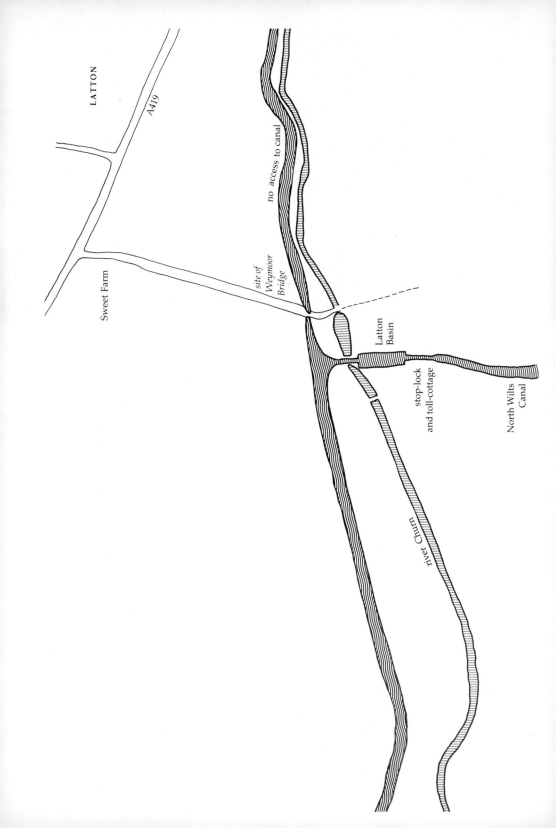

LATTON

A419

Sweet Farm

no access to canal

site of
Weymoor
Bridge

Latton
Basin

stop-lock
and toll-cottage

North Wilts
Canal

river Churn

forms an interesting comparison with the canal milestones we have been studying so far.

By following this section of main road, we have left the canal over to our right, where its infilled line can hardly be made out until it turns towards the road to cross at Latton Bridge. Not surprisingly, this was one of the first levelling operations following the canal's abandonment, and it is now very difficult to appreciate the layout of this area in canal days. The site is actually just beyond the two cottages on the left and the remains of the turning basin on the left of the road now form part of the cottage gardens.

At this same point the dual-carriageway of the Cricklade by-pass begins, and the old line of canal is totally obliterated. In fact, its route was parallel with what remains of the former road and this latter is the recommended route down to the wharf. Midway along – and on the left of the old road – stood Latton Lock with a fall of 9' 4". It has vanished completely. Along this stretch we might well be forgiven for assuming that restoration of the canal is now impossible, and of course the new by-pass constitutes a major barrier. However it may well be that restoration east of the Water Park follows a totally different line from the original route, perhaps using part of the river Churn, a cattle underpass beneath the new road and a linkage into the river Thames. Already proposals have been published to improve the existing rights of navigation into Cricklade along the Thames by the introduction of three new locks above Lechlade. Although success in a venture of this kind will require the support of a large number of public and private bodies, the discussion is already under way and will doubtless take its course.

58. 'Old Willum' again, one of the last of the lengthmen on the Thames &
Severn Canal. Duties included towpath clearance as well as regular checks on
water levels etc.

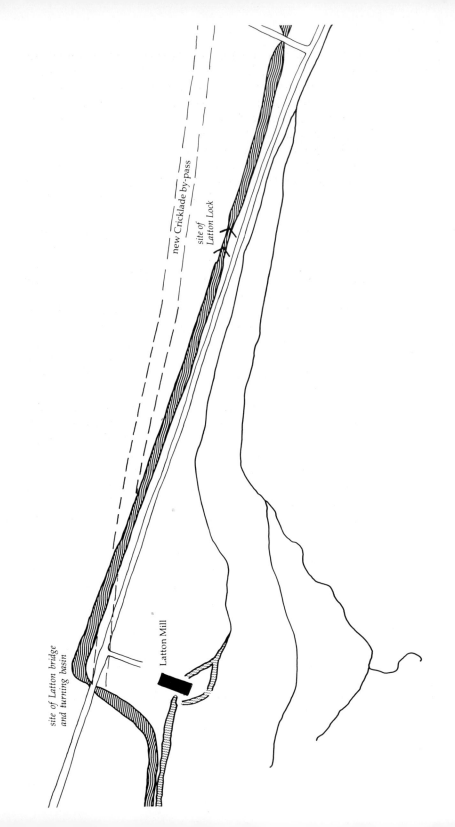

site of Latton bridge
and turning basin

Latton Mill

new Cricklade by-pass

site of
Latton Lock

Approaching Cricklade (although the canal never entered the town) the most outstanding feature is Cricklade Wharf, now the best preserved of the three examples of this particular design, and certainly better situated for study now that the new by-pass has taken all the main road traffic away from it. The site, now Wharf Farm, has enjoyed something of a rehabilitation in recent years with the owners, Mr. & Mrs. Cleaver, re-roofing the building and renewing the stucco work on the façade. Perhaps the new chocolate, coffee and cream colour scheme may not appeal to all tastes but it certainly gives the building an impact when seen, as most people do see it, from the by-pass immediately across the field.

The wharfhouse/warehouse, as at Cirencester and Kempsford, had at least two functions; firstly as accommodation for the wharfinger in the central part of the building and secondly as storage space for goods on either side and to the rear of the living accommodation, all under the one large roof. Despite recent alterations, the doorway access points for goods on the ground floor and first floor of each wing survive, and even without the hoists over these doorways this gives an excellent impression of the way the building was used. In plan it follows the Cirencester example very closely. Of all the other features of the wharf, small stables and a completely untouched coal ticket office still survive, each situated at separate entrances into the wharf. Other buildings on the other side of the wharf have gone, the old diamond shaped basin has been filled in and now forms a paddock in front of the buildings. *Wharf Farm is private property* but it can easily be seen from the old road behind and from the now truncated road alongside. The new road alignment has created a number of parking places although access to them is not from the by-pass but rather the long way round through the town of Cricklade. However a footpath now goes alongside the wharf buildings from the old road and reaches the new by-pass where a signpost indicates 'Eisey 1' across the road.

The new road is a barrier to the canal in several ways, as we have seen, but it also marks the end of the more easily walked sections of the eastern half of the canal. From here towards Inglesham it becomes more difficult to walk some sections, public rights of way are sadly reduced, and some landowners are understandably reluctant to allow free access across their land. Once across the by-pass it is easy to appreciate these points. The footpath sign reads 'Ampney Book ¾ mile', but the towpath is very overgrown, unpleasantly dominated by a thorn hedge all the way down to Eisey and is impassable. The Ampney Brook was crossed by a small aqueduct but all that remains are brick abutments and a wooden footbridge over the stream.

Access: it is best now to make more use of the car and take an alternative route to Eisey using the minor road through to Marston

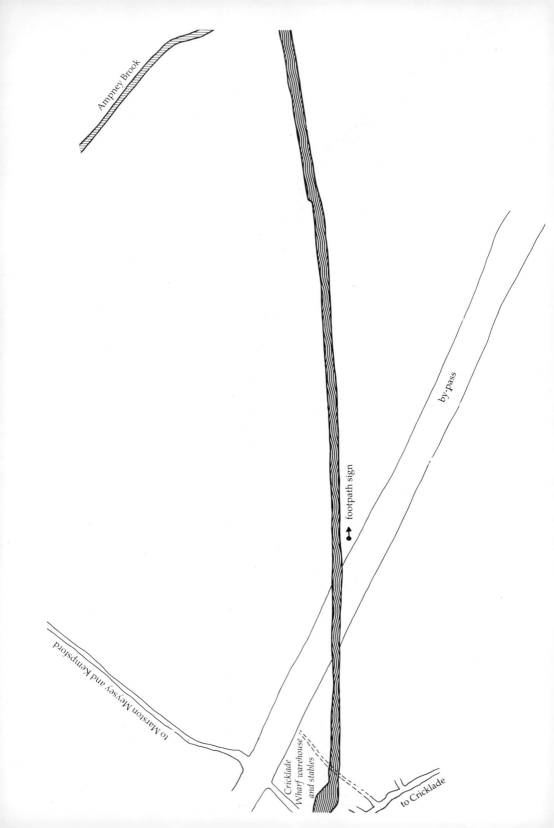

Ampney Brook

by-pass

footpath sign

to Marston Meysey and Kempsford

Cricklade
Wharf warehouse
and stables

to Cricklade

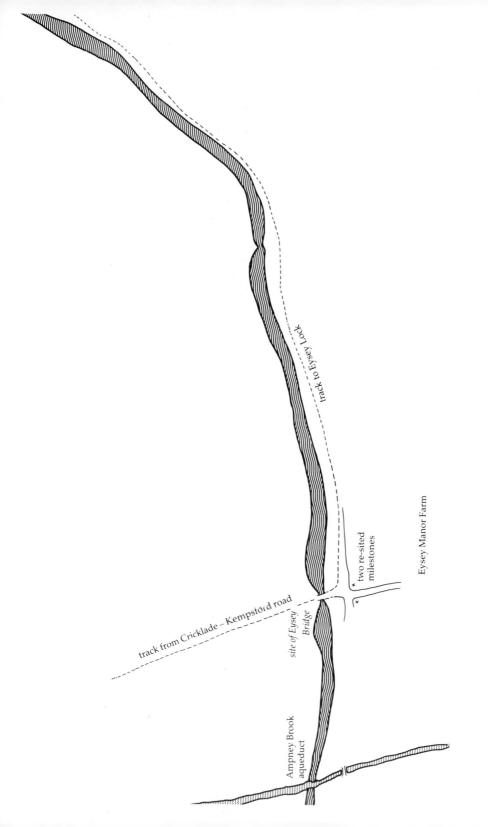

track to Eysey Lock

two re-sited
milestones

Eysey Manor Farm

track from Cricklade – Kempsford road

site of Eysey
Bridge

Ampney Brook
aqueduct

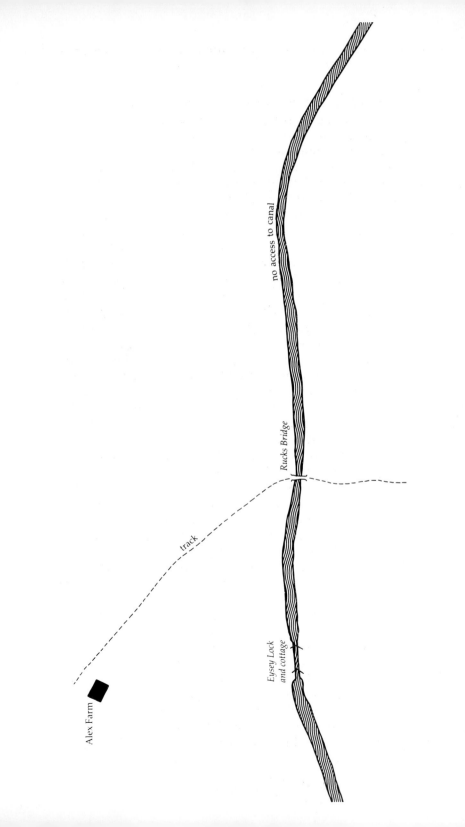

no access to canal

Rucks Bridge

track

Eysey Lock
and cottage

Alex Farm

Meysey and Kempsford which leaves the by-pass just a few yards from the footpath. This road will give access to all the points of contact between here and Kempsford.

The first right hand turn off this road signposted 'Eysey Only' leads down a half mile track towards Eysey Manor and farm. The canal bridge just before the farm has been levelled and the canal route to either side of it is very overgrown. Limited parking is possible here for exploration but the most striking features are the two milestones restored at either side of the farm entrance. Both are complete with plates showing WALBRIDGE 22 INGLESHAM $6\frac{3}{4}$ and WALBRIDGE $22\frac{1}{2}$ INGLESHAM $6\frac{1}{4}$. The milestones were brought here from their original positions further down the canal and because of this both have survived in good condition. By walking back towards Cricklade a short way with its distinctive church tower in the distance, the impassable line of the towpath coming across the field can best be appreciated. Here the canal crossed the Ampney Brook where the nearby cottage has been restored.

From Eysey Farm entrance a track leads off to the east alongside the canal but not on the towpath as this is too overgrown; within half a mile, or about twenty minutes pleasant walking, access to Eysey Lock and cottage can be made. The whole area is very overgrown and the cottage comes as a complete surprise; of all the isolated buildings along the canal this must be the most isolated of them all and can only now be reached by the route we have taken, or in earlier years by using the canal. The cottage has no services and remains much as it was left many years ago. It has now become increasingly derelict and must be treated with great care, but perhaps this isolation has saved it from the total destruction that has occurred at Wilmoreway cottage. Its style and history follows the same pattern as Wilmoreway as both were built in 1831 to house lengthsmen redeployed to more important duties, the man here being moved up from Marston Meysey. The cottage seems small but inside was a two-up, two-down arrangement; in the basement, built into the canal bank were two stable/storage rooms reached by an outside door. Close by is Eysey Lock which is very overgrown but still retains its bottom gates. Beyond, the canal becomes increasingly difficult to follow and a return to Eysey Farm along the track is recommended.

From the Kempsford road, the next point of contact which might be made, again down a track, is at Alex Farm, through the farm yard and down to the canal at Rucks Bridge (*a private track – please ask at the farm*). This is a large red brick built accommodation bridge where the parapets have been pushed over to allow access for modern (and wider) farm machinery over the canal. But at least the bridge still stands, when so many others have been levelled completely. This whole section from here to Marston Meysey is very isolated and there are no further points of interest along it. The next point of contact with the canal should be at

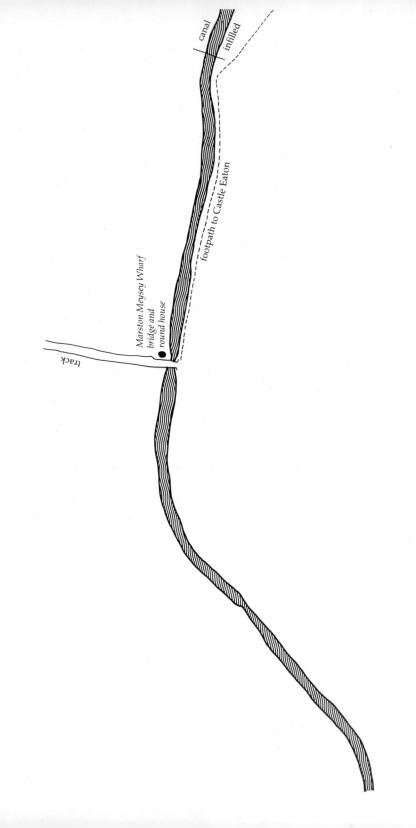

track

Marston Meysey Wharf
bridge and
round house

footpath to Castle Eaton

canal

infilled

Marston Meysey Wharf where there was another roundhouse. From the road look across the fields to the right just beyond the left hand turning to the village of Marston Meysey, and the roundhouse will clearly be seen. A farm track which is also a public footpath signposted to Castle Eaton will give access to this area which was once a tiny country wharf. Today it is virtually impossible to appreciate the optimism of the canal proprietors in establishing such remote wharves but we must remember that they were intended to serve the local community over a widely scattered rural area which was equally cut off from the alternative road system.

The bridge is a splendid survival, almost intact in red brick with a grand shape and still retaining its concrete coping. For many years the roundhouse (number four on our list) was allowed to become increasingly derelict. Some years ago it was taken in hand, the doorways and windows blocked up and the exterior re-cemented to protect the stonework from the elements. The roof replacement faithfully follows the original inverted principle recorded at Coates roundhouse. Inside, all floors have gone, but as least the building survives. Its basic function, position alongside the canal and its history follow that of the other three roundhouses we have already seen.

The wharf is otherwise largely obliterated now that a track has been put across it to give access to the fields beyond. This leaves the bridge unused, which might well be its saviour for the future. Careful inspection along the approach track to the site will reveal the remains of a pair of stone pillars, which when hung with their gates, as at all wharves, must have given this remote spot a touch of grandeur. To either side the canal has been filled in and it is easy to see how complete has been the return to agriculture of this part of the eastern section. There is hardly a depression in the ground or a different colouration in the cultivated soil to mark the canal route, and a return to the road is now necessary in order to proceed towards Kempsford.

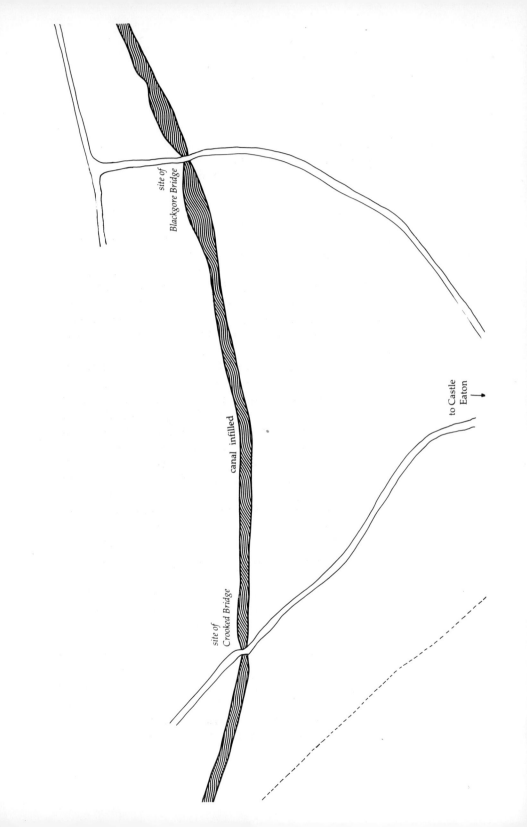

site of
Blackgore Bridge

canal infilled

site of
Crooked Bridge

to Castle
Eaton

CHAPTER SIXTEEN

Marston Meysey to Lechlade

Our final section is the most difficult to follow and relatively little of it will be seen. There are indeed less points of interest than elsewhere, and this is one of the reasons why a return to agricultural use has been possible for much of the remainder of the line to Inglesham.

The next two small roads through to Castle Eaton both went over the canal via Crooked Bridge and Blackgore Bridge both of which were levelled many years ago. Only the presence of red bricks in the hedgerows and a small rise in the road levels reveal where they used to be as the canal bed to either side has been filled. Our next point of contact with the canal is at Oatlands Bridge, an accommodation bridge to the land between the canal and River Thames, and this stands in splendid isolation over in the field opposite the Dunfield turning. It was not levelled because of the wishes of the owner some years ago and can be inspected freely and at leisure. As with other features along the canal that remain in isolation, its appearance must raise questions in the minds of those who are unaware that a canal once came through here. Note the stamped brick, Stonehouse Brick and Tile Co. Ltd., built into the parapet, which shows that bricks were being brought up the canal from established brick works far away to complete these bridges. On either side of the bridge the canal bed has been filled in and only the imagination can now recall the canal scene laid out below.

With Kempsford church tower prominent to the east, the rest of the canal route is without further interest apart from the site of a Swing Bridge behind the Green in Kempsford, giving access to the land between the canal and the river Thames. One other point to make about these filled sections here is that both milestones were removed for safe keeping and are both preserved, complete with their mileage plates, elsewhere in the village.

Our next point of access is at Kempsford Wharf. This is reached by travelling through the village; just past the George Inn there is a small road off to the right called Wharf Lane, which leads past a row of red brick cottages to the entrance pillars of the Wharf. The pillars still have a pair of old wooden gates and the whole area remains *private property with no right of access*. Immediately beside the entrance is a very small

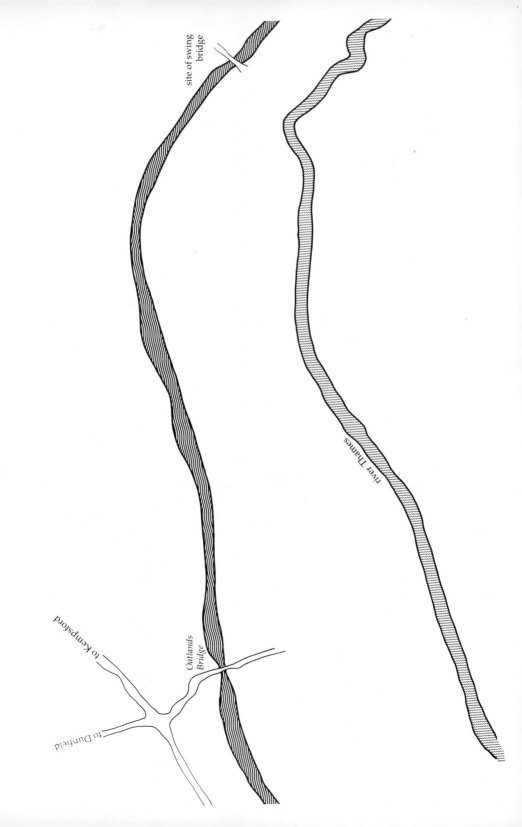

site of swing
bridge

river Thames

to Kempsford

Oatlands
Bridge

to Dunfield

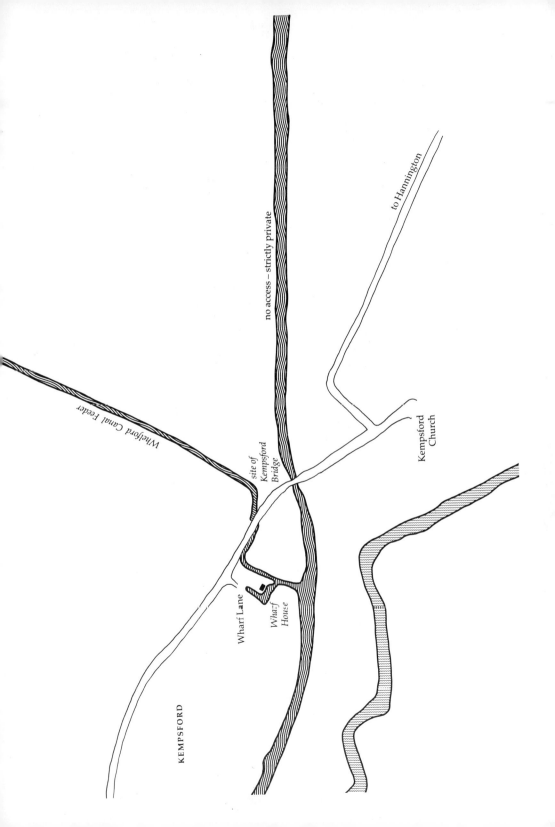

no access – strictly private

to Hannington

Whelford Canal Feeder

site of
Kempsford
Bridge

Kempsford Church

Wharf Lane

Wharf
House

KEMPSFORD

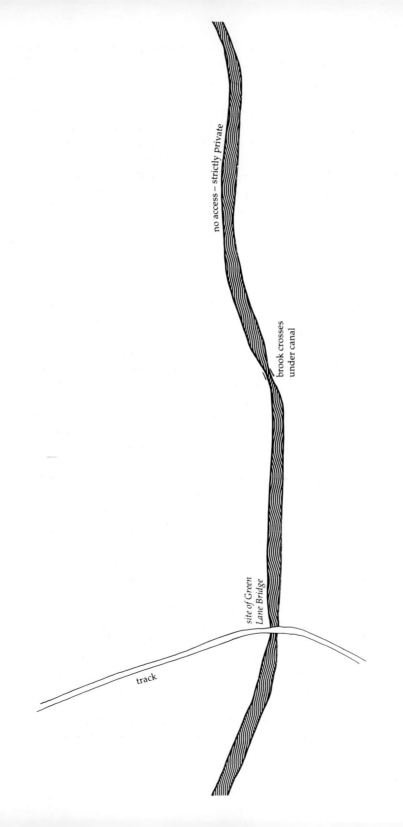

no access – strictly private

brook crosses
under canal

site of Green
Lane Bridge

track

whitewashed cottage which was the 'beer house' for the wharf serving its beer through a hatch between the buildings. On the wharf remains the ticket office, various cart sheds, stables and storage sheds, with the main wharfingers/warehouse building called Wharf House. This building is to the same design as at Cirencester and Cricklade and served the same purpose but it is a narrower building. Externally it survives almost untouched and well deserves to be preserved for its history alone. The wharf stretches down to the canal and has a few large trees on it. To the left and now infilled was the canal feeder for this section down to Inglesham; called the Whelford feeder this was taken from the outflow at Whelford Mill, the last mill on the river Coln about two miles away. It made its way across the flat land of the Thames Valley and with only a small drop in level needed constant clearing out to maintain the flow. It proved to be a very valuable feeder supplying the Double Lock at Dudgrove and the Inglesham Junction into the Thames, a combined fall of almost eighteen feet.

From the wharf the canal curved to the humped-back Kempsford Bridge, now levelled to make traffic flow easier through the village, and from here the route crosses open countryside devoid of houses until it joins the Thames three miles away. At Kempsford the canal and Thames are only a hundred yards apart and many proposals were put forward suggesting a linkage into the Thames either here or at Dudgrove; all of them were shelved. From Kempsford Bridge the canal route is *strictly private property and this must be respected*. There are no remains of interest as far as Green Lane Bridge, where access can be made by taking the Hannington road out of Kempsford and after about half-a-mile turning down a grassy track on the left. This leads to the levelled bridge site from which it can be seen that the filled canal route is marked only by the original position of the hedgerow coming across from Kempsford.

As for the rest, it is sufficient to say that the line survives along the next section but points of interest are few and far between, and there is no public access. A small brook crosses deep under the canal with a long masonry waist above it, almost giving the impression of a wharf but the line is very overgrown and completely isolated from houses and roads. The canal swings to the north-east to avoid Brazen Church Hill, isolated some three hundred feet high, but even then it has to enter a deep cutting into which it has been tiered down as it approaches Hamfield Bridge. The arching has half collapsed into the canal and it will not be long before the whole structure falls down. All types of wild birds flourish along these reaches, which seem to hold water fairly well due probably to the clayey soil through which the line is cut. A more understandable reason for the wildlife is the complete lack of human intrusion. Returning into Kempsford take the road out to Whelford, where the feeder now runs along in front of the houses on the left as you

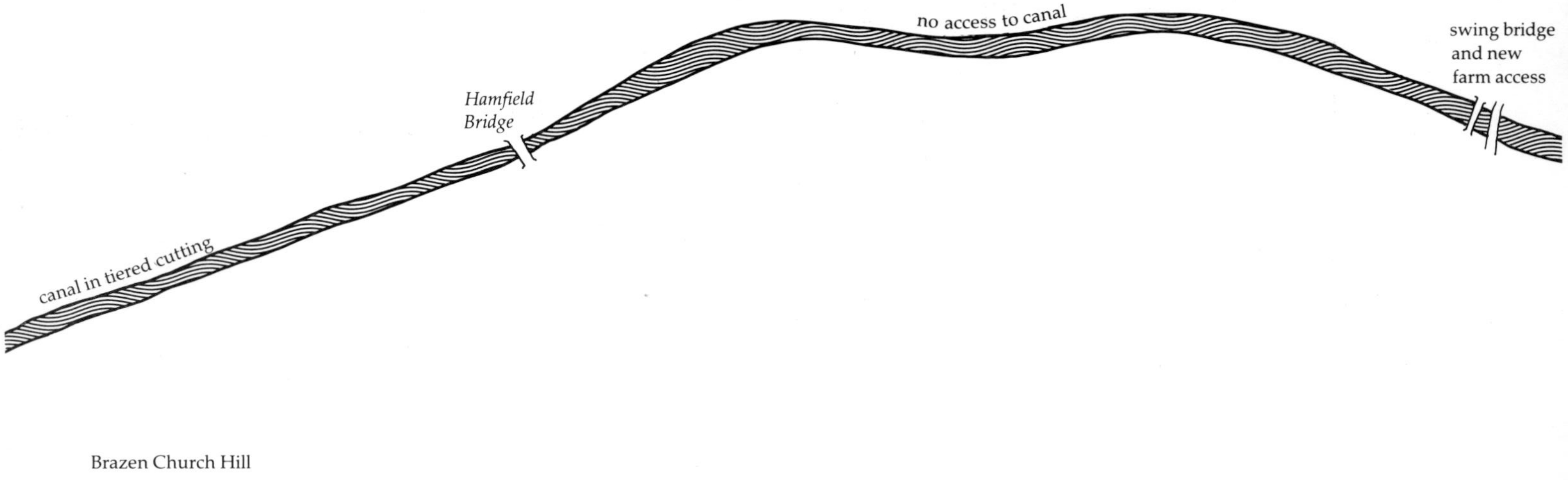

swing bridge
and new
farm access

no access to canal

Hamfield
Bridge

canal in tiered cutting

Brazen Church Hill

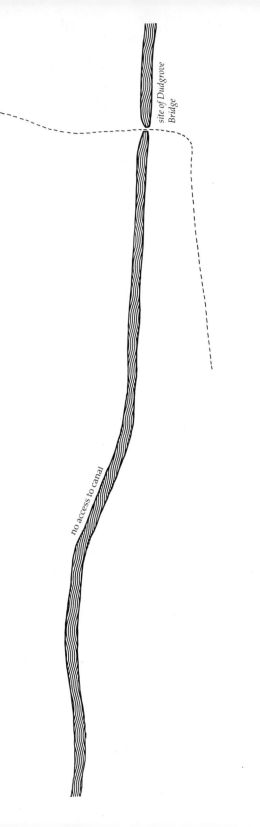

Dudgrove
Farm

site of Dudgrove
Bridge

no access to canal

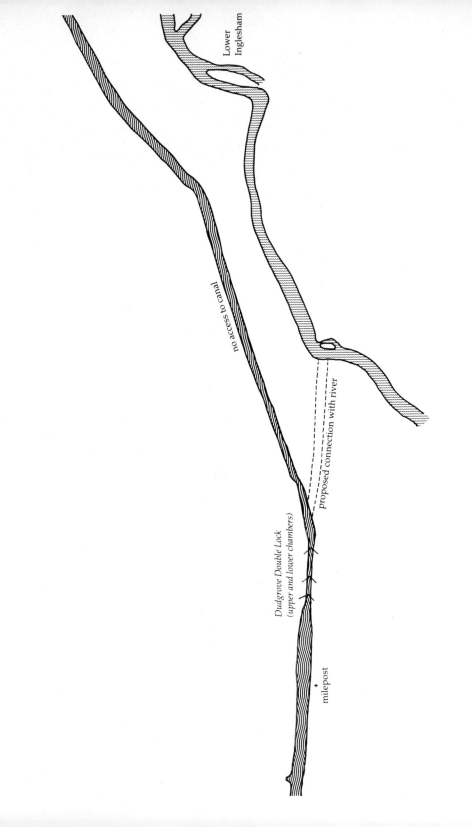

Lower
Inglesham

no access to canal

proposed connection with river

Dudgrove Double Lock
(upper and lower chambers)

milepost

enter Whelford. The course has mainly been filled in but further along the road at Popes Corner the feeder ditch is still open but carries no water now. It follows round a bend in the road to cross under just before Whelford Mill. By looking down into the river from the bridge here the arch taking the feeder out of the mill race can be seen over in the wall of the house. Just past the bridge will be seen the signpost to 'Dudgrove Only' off to the right. Follow this road until it comes into the yard of Dudgrove Farm where *with permission* it is possible to walk on down the track to the site of Dudgrove Bridge, now levelled for agricultural access.

Above this bridge the canal line survives from Hamfield Bridge to the west although now very overgrown. A swing bridge still remains but it has now settled onto the canal bed, so that access across the canal is now by a track alongside. From Dudgrove Bridge it is possible to turn left along a track, alongside the canal, which soon ends just short of Dudgrove Double Lock. *Access to this isolated and dangerous spot must be obtained from Dudgrove Farm.* The milepost just above the locks still survives and its mileage plate WALBRIDGE 28 INGLESHAM ¾ was removed in 1959 to the Waterways Museum at Stoke Bruerne. There are no other points of interest on this section which makes its way across isolated land, devoid of houses and road, in a north easterly direction to reach the lock.

Dudgrove Double Lock is the only example of its type on the whole length of the Thames & Severn. The upper chamber is a normal red brick deep lock with a 9' fall and typical of so many locks along the line. However, it leads directly into a roughly-built lower chamber con-

59. Dudgrove Double Lock in the middle of fields near Lechlade, seen here in 1896. The combined fall was 11 feet 6 inches.

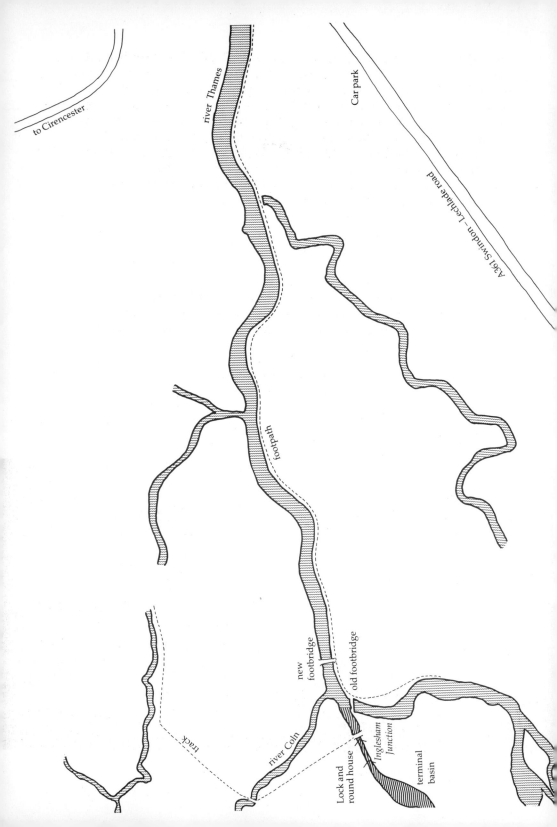

to Cirencester

river Thames

Car park

A361 Swindon – Lechlade road

footpath

track

river Coln

new footbridge

old footbridge

Inglesham Junction

Lock and round house

terminal basin

structed of loose stone walling with only a 2' 6" fall. The story behind this is an interesting one. The canal had been built this far by the early months of 1789 but this final section to join the Thames had yet to be agreed or even marked out on the ground. The cause of the dispute was the state of the upper reaches of the river, a notoriously ill-kept section and difficult for navigation. Fearful of achieving so much and then running into problems of this kind, the canal proprietors sought alternative solutions, including even a direct cut from Dudgrove to Abingdon. This reminds us very forcibly of the solution later offered to this same problem by the alternative North Wilts and Wilts & Berks routes to Abingdon, and helps to explain the willingness of the Thames & Severn authorities to dispense so readily with the whole of this eastern section in due course. But the problem in the year in which the canal was opened was indeed a pressing one, and the only solution was to cut the approved line to join the river at Inglesham. This meant that at Dudgrove a further fall was required, hence the afterthought which the lower lock represents. The nature of its construction also suggests that perhaps hopes lingered for a better solution and a new line in due course.

At this point the river is very close and remains so as far as Inglesham. The actual point of contact with the river was also under discussion; a junction at Inglesham avoided the shallow stretches known to exist immediately above, and was also of course the junction of the rivers Coln and Thames, thus ensuring deeper waters. At the upper chamber remains of the gates include the bottom pair almost closed, but they are

60. Roundhouse, lock and bridge at Inglesham where the T & S reaches the River Thames. From a print of 1793

very decayed and the balance beams have collapsed onto the lockside. In the lower chamber the rough unmortared sloping sides are in complete contrast to any other lock masonry along the canal; again the bottom gates are still in position but very decayed. It must be said that both chambers remain in good condition. Having explored these two locks a return up the track to Dudgrove Farm is now necessary, leaving the canal heading off to the north-east where it is crossed by a farm access track and also by a drainage ditch cut completely through the canal bed. This length remains full of reeds and the towpath is impassable.

The final point of contact with the canal can be made by driving into Lechlade and parking in the Market Place, where there are several inns and tea shops for refreshments before a final look at this part of the waterway. Walk back up to Thames Street, the main A361 road to Swindon, and up onto Lechlade Bridge over the river where it is possible to survey the river scene and the area of the Parkend Wharf laid out below. The road traffic, the river boats and the summer hordes of people are all in stark contrast to the tranquil scenes we have been used to along virtually all the rest of the waterway. There is access to another, and the original, access point into Parkend Wharf by walking from the Market Place to Bell Lane just past Thames Street; there is direct public access too from Thames Street, so a good look around this busy area can be made. The Wharf obviously does not represent its old self and where

61. Inglesham group of buildings seen from the River Thames approach from Lechlade. The river turns off to the left, the canal enters the lock just beyond the bridge. Roundhouse and warehouse in the centre. Photographed after the canal's closure in 1927.

once barges tied up to unload coal, stone and agricultural products etc. cabin cruisers are stored and repaired. Certain of the old wharf buildings have survived, basically unaltered; the two most important being the warehouse and the agent's house behind it. The former is now a restaurant and shop whilst the agent's house has been converted into flats. The stone block edging to the wharf on the river is still basically unchanged but is now hung with rubber tyres to protect the paintwork of the boats.

In order to get to Inglesham Junction walk up the left hand bank upstream along the river, with access from the side of Lechlade Bridge. In something over half-a-mile this will bring you to the junction buildings on the opposite side of the river. The public right of way then crosses over the newly positioned footbridge just before the bend in the river at which both canal and River Coln enter the Thames on the opposite bank. Walk up to the bend to look across at the Inglesham buildings noting the old position of the towpath and footbridge from the remaining abutments on either bank. This right of way no longer exists

62. 1896 view of Inglesham, looking particularly bleak and exposed. Even so, the shape of both bridge and roundhouse remain a distinctive feature of the Thames & Severn Canal's architecture.

221

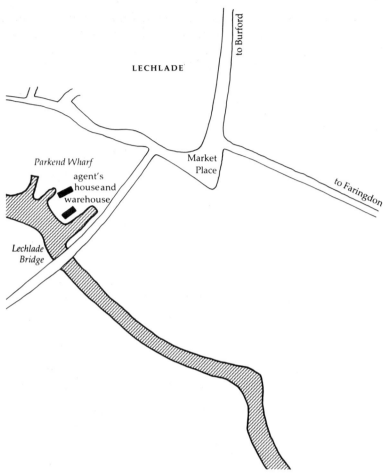

and to protect the privacy of the owners at Inglesham the path has been moved to its present site. *The site remains private property* but the main features can be described. Above the lock the terminal basin survives, which was also used as a turning pound for barges. Inglesham Lock with a 6' fall brings the canal down to the level of the Thames and remains in good condition as does the bridge over the tail of the lock. This bears the date November 14 1789, just five days before the first boat passed through the canal and into the Thames. The roundhouse is the fifth and last along the canal and is in very good condition as is the small warehouse close to it, both now used as private houses. The final milestone, complete with its mileage plate, was moved off the towpath into the yard of the roundhouse some years ago. It records that the journey from Stroud has covered $28\frac{1}{2}$ miles, to which should be added the $1\frac{1}{4}$ mile arm into Cirencester – a total of a little less than thirty miles from Stroud to Lechlade.

Access to Inglesham can also be gained from a track off the A417 Fairford – Lechlade road just before you enter Lechlade and signposted 'Unsuitable for Motor Vehicles'. It can certainly be walked and provides an alternative route back into Lechlade. Otherwise return by retracing one's steps back along the river bank.

Further Reading

Freeman Fox Braine & Partners *Feasibility Report* on the restoration of through navigation on the Stroudwater Navigation and Thames & Severn Canal, Cardiff 1976.

Handford, Michael *The Stroudwater Canal* Alan Sutton, 1979.

Household, Humphrey *The Thames & Severn Canal* new edition, Alan Sutton, 1983.

Inland Waterways Association (IWA), Oxford and South Bucks branch Feasibility Study on the *Higher Thames Improvement for Navigation*, 1981.

Lewis, Christopher three articles on Josiah Clowes 1735–94 in *Waterways World*, April and May 1978 and May 1980.

Poole, John *Saul Adam* Thornhill Press, Gloucester, 1973

Roberts, Trevor *A Canal Walk Through Stroud* Stroudwater, Thames & Severn Canal Trust 1982. Covers Eastington to Sapperton.

Rowles, Wilf 'Built at Brimscombe Port' *Waterways World* March 1978, pages 52-7. Studies the boat-building yard of Abdela & Mitchell.

Shipman, Juliet *Chalford Place* privately published in 1979; 16pp; a history of the house (latterly the Company's Arms) and its clothier families.

Stroudwater Thames & Severn Canal Trust Ltd. official magazine *The Trow*, issued quarterly; covers current Trust matters, activities and plans together with historical articles etc. Trust membership details from Hon. Secretary, No. 1 Riveredge, Framilode, Glos. (Tel: Gloucester 740525).

Tann, Jennifer *Gloucestershire Woollen Mills* David & Charles, Newton Abbot 1967. Remains the standard reference work.

Thurston, E. Temple *The Flower of Gloster* David & Charles 1968. New illustrated edition, Alan Sutton 1984.

Viner, David *The Thames & Severn Canal: a survey from historical photographs* Hendon Publishing Co., 1975.

Viner, David 'The Thames & Severn Canal in Cirencester' in *Studies in the archaeology and history of Cirencester*, Oxford 1976, pp.126-44.

Viner, David 'On the threshold of darkness: canal tunnel restoration in Gloucestershire' *Country Life*, 18 January 1979, pp.162-3.

Acknowledgements

The preparation of a volume of this kind requires the support and active assistance of many people and both authors are extremely grateful for the support they have received from a wide variety of sources, not all of which can be mentioned here.

We are particularly indebted to David and Margaret Boakes and members of the Trust Council for their continuing support, and to Iris Capps, James Clark, Colin Downes, Norman Ferry, Peter Gadsden, Geoffrey Martin, Raymond Tudor, John Stephens and Stanley White. The work of Charles Hadfield has been a constant source of inspiration, and Humphrey Household's major study of the Thames & Severn Canal remains a 'bible' in both our hands. Eddie Cuss has made freely available of his own knowledge and researches into aspects of local canal history, not least a survey of the milestones on the Thames & Severn Canal, and he has contributed substantially to this volume. In characteristic style, Frederick Rowbotham, Lionel Walrond, Stan Gardiner, Syd Matthews and David Boakes have all given freely of their time and generously of their knowledge and advice.

The plans of Carter's Close on page 32 and Kemmett's Canal on page 58 are reproduced by courtesy of the Company of Proprietors of the Stroudwater Navigation. GCRO D1180 10/3, and GCRO D1180 10/1.

SOURCE OF PHOTOGRAPHS

For photographs 1 to 18 *Michael Handford collection*; for 19, *Corinium Museum, Cirencester* (courtesy Dr. P.H. Bright, Minchinhampton); 20, 48, 52, 56, 59 and 62, *Hugh McKnight collection*; 21, 22, 25, 32 and 34, *Stan Gardiner, France Lynch* (from various sources); 23, (from Storer & Brewer *Delineations of Gloucestershire* 1826); 29, 30, 33 and 42, *Humphrey Household collection*; 24, *David McDougall collection*; 26 and 47, *Frank Lloyd, Gloucester*; 27, 31, (Frith & Co.), 40, 46, 51 and 55, *Gloucestershire Record Office*; 35, *John Stanley, Cirencester* (courtesy Mrs. P. Sullivan); 36, 38, 39, 43 and 54, *National Monuments Record* (courtesy Oxford City Library); 37 and 60, *Stroudwater Thames & Severn Canal Trust*; 41, from an original by *W. Dennis Moss, Cirencester*; 44 and 50, *Chris Bowler and Abbey Studios, Cirencester*; 45, *A.F Kersting*; 49, *Reece Winstone*; 53, *South Cerney Local History Society*; 57, 58, *Michael Ware collection* (courtesy Mrs. Temple Thurston); 61, *Wilts & Glos Standard, Cirencester*.

The map on page 2 has been drawn by Bob Zeepvat who is also responsible for the drawings on pages 157 and 162, the latter from an original measured drawing by Richard Warmington.